P9-CNI-877

THE
SECOND HALF
OF CREATION

AN EXPLANATION OF
THE MISSION OF JESUS

Patrick J. Amer

Copyright © 2003 by Patrick J. Amer.

ISBN: Softcover   1-4134-1780-9

All rights reserved. No part of this book may be reproduced or transmitted in any form or by any means, electronic or mechanical, including photocopying, recording, or by any information storage and retrieval system, without permission in writing from the copyright owner.

This book was printed in the United States of America.

To order additional copies of this book, contact:
Xlibris Corporation
1-888-795-4274
www.Xlibris.com
Orders@Xlibris.com
20151

THE
SECOND HALF
OF CREATION

Praise for
THE SECOND HALF OF CREATION

"I have been telling everyone how impressed I am with your manuscript. It is beautifully written. It is so clear that I had to reread only one sentence in the entire piece, and that was probably a result of my getting distracted. . . . I found your arguments convincing, especially about sacrifice, the purpose of the second half of creation and prayer. I will have to think much more in depth about Christ's God-consciousness. . . . Your treatment on why Christ came when he did was the first time I ever heard a good explanation of why. . . . Chapter 6 on the mission is compelling. . . . I find your entire topic unusually relevant today, particularly in light of the questions in today's newspaper articles on the authoritarian, arrogant Roman Catholic Church." - J. G.

"Your manuscript came to me at a very important time in my life. Although I've been a practicing Catholic for many years (I'm a convert), the concept of original sin has never made any sense to me. That along with questions about papal infallibility led me to read Thomas Cahill's book about Pope John XXIII plus his "How the Irish Saved Civilization." In my mind, Cahill's books opened the door and yours took it right off the hinges!! . . . In summary let me say that your book has helped me on the road to becoming a much better Christian, and I'm really looking forward to the trip. . . . I really liked the way you summarized the teachings of Jesus and how we can strive to live by them." -J. R.

"What I find the strongest and truest about your book are the passages where you are clearly narrating for the reader the intellectual path you have been following as you have synthesized your personal religious and educational experiences, your legal expertise, with your readings in cultural studies, theology, history, biology and with your understanding of the life which you have experienced." - D. A.

"You are on track with thoughts that I have had and have wondered why are not presented as explanations or theories. It is interesting and gratifying for me to read your in-depth thoughts which are based on much reading and research and to learn there is a basis for my musings. Also, I like your writing style. Easy to read, some humor, but still on an intellectual level." - M.O.

"I believe it to be an important book – perhaps a major book. . . . Powerful and brilliant words. . . . The idea of free will superbly described. . . . I suggest you try and get this into print as soon as possible. It's going to be a road to Damascus book for some. And the time is now! A lot of people are querying religion and God after September 11 and the ongoing war and the morality of a pre-emptive strike against Iraq. Your studies and thoughts could make a real contribution. I'm sure you have the balance right now and I'm bullish about its success." - J.B.

"Amer's argument is cogent, well-reasoned, and supported by carefully-researched historical data. You will certainly change your thinking after reading this book. You may even change your life." - B.P.

"I read it from cover to cover and kept thinking, 'Why couldn't I see that before?'. . . . The culture of sacrifice and its tie in with evolution was one of the clearest analyses I have ever read to reconcile my faith with outward appearances of the material world. Do not change a word. . . . You provide a method to make sense of both concepts. . . . Your book has allowed me to make a little more out of my existence than I had before I read it. I hope that you publish it soon, as I intend to share it with the thinking people I know." - T.R.

FOR MY PARENTS
GRACE O'HARA AMER
AND
FRANCIS JOSEPH AMER
WHO FIRST INTRODUCED ME
TO CHRISTIAN THEOLOGY
AND TO LIFE

"Violence rests on the assumption that the enemy and I are entirely different: the enemy is evil and I am good. But love sees things differently. It sees that even the enemy suffers from the same sorrows and limitations that I do. That we both have the same hopes, the same needs, the same aspirations for a peaceful and harmless human life. And that death is the same for both of us."
Thomas Merton

"FRANGO UT PATEFACIAM."
Motto of the Paleontological Society

TABLE OF CONTENTS.

INTRODUCTION.

"Why did Jesus come? What exactly did he come to do?" These are old questions. But the old answers are increasingly seen to be inadequate, and the old questions are being asked again with renewed concern. To answer these questions, I propose an explanation of the mission of Jesus which varies in many ways from the orthodox Roman Catholic or Protestant explanations. I believe it is coherent, satisfying and persuasive. I believe it answers many questions and sheds light on many problems not successfully dealt with by present teaching of the Christian Churches. The purpose of this book is to set forth this explanation.

I was brought up in a devout Catholic family. I received about as much Catholic education as one can get, and I have read a great deal of philosophy and theology on my own. After graduating from a Jesuit university I went to law school, and I have been a practicing lawyer for almost four decades. In the 1960s and 1970s, I drifted away from religious practice, and then from religious conviction, as did so many of my contemporaries. I saw the Roman Catholic Church miss the civil rights movement, ignore the anti-Vietnam War movement, and begin its repudiation of the reforms of the Second Vatican Council (1962-65) which continues to this day. On a more fundamental level, I felt a profound disconnect between the teachings of the Christian Churches and the culture of the real world, the modern world. The Christian Churches seemed to me to be addressing the modern world in language and with concepts from a different century. Many of these teachings were not harmful; they were just not relevant.

I have continued to be interested in religious thought and its development, and I have read widely in such spare time as I have had. For some time I pursued the study of comparative mythology, principally in the books of Joseph Campbell. For a while it seemed to me that Campbell had succeeded in describing Christianity as just one part of the larger pattern and structure of the great mythologies of mankind. As will appear, I no longer think this is the case. Indeed, I have come to believe precisely the opposite: Christianity is in fundamental opposition to the culture of the great mythologies. I do accept the teaching of Campbell and others that the great mythologies have been important forces in the development of human culture, and that a statement of one's religious convictions must address and deal with the natural religions of mankind (which I call the "culture of sacrifice") as preserved and described in the classic mythologies. My explanation of Jesus's mission does so.

Though I am no scientist, I have read a number of good non-technical descriptions of modern science, particularly those that deal with the evolution and emergence of life and human behavior. I believe that anyone setting forth an explanation of the mission of Jesus today must take into account the discoveries of modern biology and anthropology, and I intend to do so.

It seems to me, looking back, that my discovery of the explanation of the mission of Jesus set forth in this book was preceded by a long period during which I "deconstructed" some of the traditional teachings of the Christianity I was taught in church and school. It always seems to take longer to strip old walls and woodwork of layers of paint and wallpaper than it does to varnish and paint the original natural wood and plaster, once cleaned and restored. Similarly, I have found that rejecting an erroneous or misleading idea, and pursuing the implications of that rejection, has sometimes been more difficult and has often taken me longer than discovering the truth which replaced it. And as any home handyman knows, once you start stripping woodwork, the job always grows and takes more time and effort than you originally thought it would. Some readers may feel that in some of the following pages I have hammered away at theological positions I have rejected with greater force than necessary. My own experience has led me to conclude that getting rid of misleading or erroneous concepts is often the harder part of the mental work necessary to see what is true. For this reason I have put the motto of the Paleontological Society on the dedication page: "*Frango ut patefaciam*"—I break in order to make clear.

Some of the traditional Christian or Catholic teachings which I have rejected, and continue to reject, are peripheral to the central doctrines of Christianity: for example, the teachings of the Roman Catholic Church on infallibility and on birth control. Two of those rejected teachings, however, are central: the Fall of Adam and Eve, and the teaching that Jesus's death was a sacrifice demanded by God to make atonement for Adam's and Eve's, and mankind's, sin.

The Christian teaching that God created humanity in a state of original perfection, that the first man and the first woman sinned, and that humans were thereafter separated from God, is in my view misleading and false. Since, as I have concluded, there was no state of original perfection, it follows that Jesus did not come to restore mankind to that original perfection. He did not come to redeem mankind from Adam's and Eve's sin.

As to the atoning sacrifice, I am not able to believe that God demanded, desired or required the torture and death of Jesus. I cannot believe that God took pleasure or found satisfaction in the death of his Son. I do not accept the Christian doctrine of "substitutionary atonement." If, as I conclude, there was no substitutionary atonement, it follows that Jesus did not take our sins upon him, and he did not come to die for our sins.

I expect that most of my readers who have given the matter any thought share my doubts and difficulties with the Christian teachings that we were all "represented" by Adam and Eve in their sin, and so we were all punished, and that we were all "represented" by Jesus in his death, and so we were all redeemed. On many levels, these teachings make no sense at all. But without them what do we make of Jesus? Why did he come, if not to redeem us from Adam's sin? What did he do that was so important, if not take on himself the sins of mankind and offer himself as a bloody human sacrifice to God? In the absence of an alternative explanation, many of us are not at all sure what the mission of Jesus was. I do not think that traditional Christian teaching has given us a satisfactory answer to the questions, "Why did Jesus come?" and "What exactly did he do?" I propose a new and different answer to these questions.

I propose that the way to understand the mission of Jesus is to take the view that God created humans in two stages, or phases. The first half of creation is God's creation of the universe in such a way as to cause the evolution of a unique species of animal with powers of self-consciousness, reflection, self-direction, communication and cooperation: the human race. The second half of creation began with God's singular intervention, in about 4 B.C., in Israel, when Jesus of Nazareth was born. The life, teaching, death and resurrection of Jesus is the second half of creation. I propose to explain first, why God chose to proceed in this way, as well as I can understand and express it, and second, how the life, teaching, death and resurrection of Jesus works the redemption and salvation of all men and women and the cleansing and renovation of the world.

I believe that the explanation I propose is fully orthodox and Christian. I still say and mean every phrase of the Apostles' Creed and the Nicene Creed, although I do not accept the neo-Platonic philosophy embedded in the latter. I accept, though from a different philosophical ground, the teaching that Jesus is both God and man; I explain this in Chapter IV.

The core of Christianity is its claim that God has redeemed humanity through Jesus Christ, and through no one else and in no other way. If God has redeemed humanity through Jesus Christ, it follows that the humanity which God created has always needed to be redeemed. The Christian needs to try to understand not only how, but why, God created humans so that they were always in need of redemption, in order to understand, accept and participate in the redemptive activity of Jesus. This book sets forth my approach to this understanding.

A quite surprising amount of theological writing about Jesus and his mission seems to ignore what Jesus himself said. I discovered my interpretation of his mission in the course of a careful reading and organization of the teachings of Jesus set forth in the Gospels. I believe that Jesus told us and showed us what he came to do; the explanation of why he came can be found in his teachings. As I see it, I am not proposing my personal understanding of his mission; I am trying to elucidate Jesus's own understanding of his mission from his own words. As Jesus said, "He that has ears to hear, let him hear." Lk 8, 8.

Many people who were brought up Catholic or Protestant have now come to think that much of what they were taught as true Christianity is childish, not thoughtful, presented as dogma rather than as the result of mature reflection, and in many ways not much help in living life or relating to the world. I know many people like this. Some are bright, well-educated and well-intentioned people who as adults have little use for Christianity. Some are good practicing Christians who just aren't sure what they now believe. Among these are some who call themselves "cafeteria Christians"; they take some of this and some of that, but they reject, or remain unsure about, much of what is taught in the name of the Christian Churches. I have lived and worked through these positions of doubt, rejection and uncertainty myself. I propose to those who hold these doubts and uncertainties an explanation of the mission of Jesus which I believe is thoughtful, mature, coherent and modern. I hope that those readers may find in this explanation some insights in the light of which they can arrive at a more coherent, satisfying and challenging understanding of their own religious beliefs.

I shall describe this explanation of the mission of Jesus in this order:

Chapter I sets forth the traditional Christian explanation of the mission and redemptive activity of Jesus, and my reasons for finding it inadequate and erroneous. Chapter II discusses the problematic behaviors of humans which are included in our genetic heritage. Chapter III treats the origin and development of the natural religions of humanity, the culture of sacrifice. Chapters II and III set forth my understanding of the first half of creation of the human race, the emergence of civilized humanity, and the nature of its need of redemption.

Chapters IV and V deal with the person and the teaching of Jesus. In Chapter IV, I attempt to explain how Jesus was truly a man, yet also truly God, and thus uniquely able to redeem and in no need of redemption himself. In Chapter V, I set forth Jesus's core teachings, and describe his understanding of his own mission as expressed in what he actually taught. Chapter VI sets forth my explanation of Jesus's mission and the nature of his redemptive activity. These three chapters are the heart of this book.

Chapter VII discusses the death and resurrection of Jesus. The remaining two chapters discuss the historic response of the Christian Churches to the teachings of Jesus, and the ways in which men and women of our day can and should respond to a correct understanding of Jesus's mission, both to receive redemption and sanctification for themselves, and to complete Jesus's redemption of the world.

I am assuming that the reader will have some familiarity with the story of Jesus as set forth in the New Testament and with the history of the Christian Churches. I have taken some of the scriptural quotations from the New Revised Standard Version, some from the Jerusalem Bible, some from the King James Version, and some from Ronald Knox's translation.

I am grateful to my sisters, Ellen Erzen and Martha Zachlin, to my brother-in-law, Bob Erzen, and to my friends, John Balfour, Barbara Patterson, Juliana Gilheany and Diane Aureden, who read my manuscript in several drafts and offered detailed and constructive criticism, to my sister-in-law Jayme Koszyn, to my good friend and law partner, Rick Taft, and to Nana Landgraf, each of whom gave me valuable suggestions and insights at critical times, and to Rev. Donald Cozzens and Joseph Kelly, who encouraged me to get this book published.

I

ANSELM'S EXPLANATION.

"Why did Jesus come?" and "What exactly did he do?" are the central questions of Christianity. I propose a new answer to these questions. Now a new answer is not needed if the traditional teaching is adequate. So I propose first to examine the traditional explanations of the mission of Jesus.

Catholic and Protestant theologians generally teach that all the historically significant explanations of Jesus's redemptive mission can be classified into three types: the deliverance or ransom theory, in which Jesus liberated humanity from bondage to the devil; the demonstration theory, in which Jesus's death was simply intended to show humanity the depths of God's love; and the theory of substitutionary atonement, which is Anselm's explanation.[1] By far the strongest and most influential of these theories is that of St. Anselm. Anselm's explanation is "still by far the most common atonement theology of the West,"[2] and because it is the theory on which many of us were brought up and which I have worked hard to exorcize, I shall concentrate on it.

First, a general observation: Jesus certainly knew why he came and what he was doing. He left with us, in the Gospels, a substantial body of speeches, sermons, parables, conversations and arguments. One would naturally expect that an explanation of his mission would be grounded in his own words and teachings.

I have found, to my astonishment, that this is not the case. The traditional Christian explanations of the mission of Jesus in general, and Anselm's explanation in particular, are theological constructs. They are almost wholly unsupported by and unrelated to the words and teachings of Jesus.

Anselm's Explanation.

The classic and probably the most cogent, concise and complete exposition of the Christian teaching about the mission of Jesus was set forth by St. Anselm of Canterbury (1033-1109). In the last decade of the eleventh century, Anselm wrote a dialogue, *Cur Deus Homo?*, or *Why Did God Become Human?*, about the mission of Jesus. Anselm's explanation may be summarized as follows:

1.   In the beginning, God created humanity, in the persons of Adam and Eve, in a state of original perfection, destined for eternal blessedness.

2.   God tested Adam's and Eve's obedience to him, and they failed the test. By their sin, not only they but all humanity with them were separated from God. As a result, all humans became unworthy of the eternal blessedness with God for which God had destined them.

3.   This separation of humanity from God, being the fault of humans, could only be repaired if humans could and would make a suitable satisfaction or atonement to God. The only appropriate atonement must take the form of a sacrifice. Since God, the offended party, is perfect, a perfect satisfaction or sacrifice was required. As all men and women were now unworthy, no human could offer a perfect sacrifice. The situation was a stalemate.

4.   God turned to Plan B. God the Father would not and apparently could not change his righteous intransigence, but God the Son took a different view, and volunteered to become a man. God the Son, in the person of Jesus, became a man, took on himself the sins of all humanity, and offered himself as an atoning sacrifice to God in his crucifixion and death.

5. As Jesus was God, the sacrifice was perfect, and thus sufficient. As he was a man, and as he had offered himself as a substitute for all humans, taking on all of the guilt of humanity, he made "substitutionary atonement" for all humans. The separation between God and humanity was closed, and all humans were redeemed.[3]

Anselm's explanation is a powerful theory. It weaves together many elements of Christian theology in a tightly-knit argument: the Genesis story of the creation of the world and the fall of Adam and Eve; the righteousness of God the Father, the God of the Old Testament; the ultimate unworthiness of humans; the mercy and love of Jesus; the importance of sacrifice in humanity's dealings with God; and the involvement of all humans in the sacrificial atonement by transfer of their guilt to Jesus. It is a complete and clever explanation. (Anselm was a clever man. It was Anselm who invented the ontological proof for the existence of God, which goes as follows: God is the supremely perfect being who possesses all positive attributes. I can conceive of such a being, so he exists in thought. But if in my thought he possesses all positive attributes, he necessarily possesses the attribute of existence. Therefore God exists. This argument has puzzled philosophers and theologians ever since.)

Rev. Rebecca Ann Parker describes the current Christian understanding of Anselm's explanation and John Calvin's development of it as follows:

> "In the beginning, human beings lived in the Garden of Eden, in perfect harmony with God. But Adam and Eve disobeyed the commandment of God. Because of their sinfulness, God had no recourse but to demand repayment for the harm they caused. We inherit their sin. The penalty for sin is death. God loves us and doesn't want to punish us. But his honor has been shamed. God is torn between love for us and the requirements of justice. To resolve this problem, he sends his only son Jesus into the world to pay

the price we owe, to bear the punishment that all of humanity deserves.

"Anselm of Canterbury formulated the first statement of this substitutionary atonement theology in the twelfth century. In *Why Did God Become Human?* Anselm said, 'No one can give himself more fully to God than when there is self-surrender to death for God's honor.'

"In the sixteenth century, John Calvin developed this theology further, placing more emphasis on the wrath and punishment of God. In his *Institutes* he said, 'Not only was Christ's body given as the price of our redemption, but he paid a greater and more excellent price in suffering in spirit the terrible torments of a condemned and forsaken man . . . . He bore the weight of divine severity, since he was "stricken and afflicted" by God's hand and experienced all the signs of a wrathful and avenging God.'

"Jesus struggles with the assignment to be our substitute. He prays, 'Father, let this cup pass from me.' But Jesus loves his father and honors the request even though it means a terrible death. Adam and Eve were disobedient, but Jesus obeys. 'Let thy will, not mine, be done.' On the cross, Jesus bears the punishment we deserve and we are set free."[4]

Anselm's explanation accurately represents current Roman Catholic and Protestant doctrine. It is stated in the Eucharistic Prayer (Rite I) in The Book of Common Prayer in this way:

"All glory be to thee, Almighty God, our heavenly Father, for that thou, of thy tender mercy, didst give thine only Son Jesus Christ to suffer death upon the cross for our redemption; who made there, by his one oblation of himself once offered, a full, perfect, and sufficient sacrifice, oblation, and satisfaction, for the sins of the whole world."

Similarly, the Catechism of the Catholic Church states that:

"Christ's death is both the Paschal sacrifice that accomplishes the definitive redemption of men, through 'the Lamb of God, who takes away the sin of the world,' and the sacrifice of the New Covenant, which restores man to communion with God by reconciling him to God through the 'blood of the covenant, which was poured out for many for the forgiveness of sins.' This sacrifice of Christ is unique; it completes and surpasses all other sacrifices. First, it is a gift from God the Father himself, for the Father handed his Son over to sinners in order to reconcile us with himself. At the same time it is the offering of the Son of God made man, who in freedom and love offered his life to his Father through the Holy Spirit in reparation for our disobedience."[5]

Problems With Anselm's Explanation.

There are many weaknesses in Anselm's explanation and in the traditional Christian doctrines which it expresses. Let us examine some of these weaknesses:

First, God did not in fact create humanity in a state of sinless perfection. The creation story in the first three chapters of Genesis is a myth. The world was not created in six days, but in something over four billion years. God did not separately create each species. Life's forms evolved by natural selection over a period of a little less than four billion years. Pre-hominids gradually evolved into humans over the last two million years. Homo Erectus could use, but hadn't learned to make, fire, half a million years ago. Homo Sapiens first appeared more than two hundred thousand years ago. There is evidence that all humans are descendants of one African woman who lived about 200,000 B.C. At what point in this long slow period of evolution "humans" appeared is impossible to determine. There must have been a first human, but who that was is unknowable.

The anthropological evidence shows that from the earliest

periods, men and their pre-human ancestors killed each other in combat.[6] Hunter-gatherer tribes were as violent and warlike as the agricultural communities which succeeded them.[7] For all prehistoric tribes, survival was a constant struggle. There was no state of original sinless perfection of humanity.

The Genesis narrative itself, read closely, does not support the traditional Christian teaching that Adam and Eve fell from a state of prior perfection when they ate the apple and sinned. In the temptation story, Adam and Eve are presented as hopelessly naive and adolescent. All of their human needs and delights were met to their full satisfaction in the Garden of Eden. They had walked with God among the trees in the evening breeze. One cannot imagine any kind of original perfection of humanity without immunity from, or at least strong powers of resistance against, temptation to sin of any kind. But we find none of that in Adam and Eve. One word from the serpent, and they ate the fruit. What the text supports is not the fall of mankind. What the text shows is that prior to the fall, Adam and Eve were all too fallible and human, and their trust in God and in his word was shallow and fickle. We can all identify with the vulnerability of Adam and Eve to temptation. This is because in the Genesis myth itself human nature is shown to be just the same before the "Fall" as it was afterward. In other words, there was no "Fall," and Adam's sin was not the "original sin."

While we are looking at the story of Adam and Eve, let us look at the nature of the command they disobeyed. God did not command them not to kill, or not to steal, or not to lie. He commanded them not to eat the fruit of a particular tree. This was a wholly arbitrary and meaningless command, a rule of dietary prohibition. When we examine the teachings of Jesus in Chapter V, we shall see what Jesus taught about meaningless and arbitrary rules, like rules of dietary prohibition, even when those rules were set forth by proper religious authorities as the commands of God.

Second, the traditional Christian teaching of the fall of mankind in Adam's sin, incorporated in Anselm's explanation, is misleading in that it implies that God had a plan for humanity, Plan A, which Adam and Eve frustrated by their sin, and that then God, in his resourcefulness, switched to Plan B, which was the redemptive life, death and resurrection of Jesus. The creation story, like all myths, treats God as if he were a king with great powers, rather than a true God. He enjoyed his Sabbath rest after six days of creation, and he liked to walk among the trees in the garden when the evening breeze sprang up. But this anthropomorphism is seriously misleading if it leads us to believe that God's plan for humanity was developed as a reaction to the action of humans, or that God became angry and cursed the earth he made, or that human mortality is a consequence of sin, or that the life of Jesus was God's fallback position, his Plan B. God is omniscient and eternal. He does not live in time. He does not react to unforeseen circumstances. He does not have a Plan B. The world we live in and experience is the world God intends and has always intended. The redemptive life, death and resurrection of Jesus was at all times God's plan for humanity.

Third, Anselm's explanation depends wholly on the assertion that the original sin, the sin of the first humans, was inherited by all humans. This notion is both unjust and pernicious. It is unjust because each person's moral relationship with God should be, and is, ultimately a matter of his or her own responsibility and his or her own conduct. The idea that the relationship between a person and God was materially and adversely altered by two other people thousands of years ago cannot be reconciled with the concept of a just, fair and benevolent God. The explanation that all men and women were "represented" by Adam and Eve is a legal fiction, and an indefensible one. One cannot delegate one's personal moral responsibility to another, or assume personal culpability and guilt for the fault of another. Even if one could, none of us ever did consent to be represented by a mythical prehistoric Adam or Eve.

The inheritability of sin is a pernicious concept as well. Once one believes that the guilt of the sin of Adam and Eve is the guilt of every man and woman, it is reasonable to believe that in general men and women can be held responsible for and can be punished for the sins of their ancestors. This is a powerful rationalization for prejudice and persecution. Even if it were true (which it is not) that the Jews of Jesus's time killed Jesus, it would not be true that later generations of Jews had any responsibility for Jesus's death. Yet many Christians throughout the last two thousand years, believing (because of the story of Adam and Eve) that sin and guilt is inheritable, have persecuted the Jews as Christ-killers.

The concept of the inheritability of sin and guilt is also bad biology. No information about the activities of a person during his or her life, or about that person's acquired character, can be transmitted from that person's body or mind to the genetic material which that person transmits to his or her offspring. This is the central dogma of molecular biology.[8] Modern science has definitively concluded that sin and guilt cannot pass from generation to generation.

While there can be no inheritance of sin and guilt, we are all aware that each of us has persistent inclinations to wrongful conduct, and persistent desires for what we cannot justly or morally take, have or enjoy. We know that resistance to and control over these inclinations and desires is difficult and necessary, and in none of us completely successful. Some of these inclinations are hereditary, in the sense that they are part of our genetic makeup. I will discuss these in Chapter II. Some are part of our culture, the environment in which we have grown up. I will discuss our cultural inheritance in Chapter III. If the Creation myth is seen as a poetic and imaginative way of describing the writer's intuitive understanding that sin, moral evil and inclinations toward wrongful conduct are always present in human life, and that mankind ought to be better, it is to that extent true. But we have no inherited responsibility or guilt for Adam's sin.

Fourth, Anselm's explanation holds that humanity's separation from God could be repaired only if humanity were able to make an acceptable payment of restitution to God, in satisfaction and atonement for humanity's sinfulness. God could not, in Anselm's understanding, simply forgive men and women for their sins; to do so would be inconsistent with God's holiness and justice. If God indiscriminately forgave sin without a satisfactory offering of restitution, he would subvert his own moral order, which God could not do.

The idea of a god who requires offerings and sacrifices from his people is common to many pagan religions. The God of the Old Testament is often this sort of God, righteous, wrathful and demanding. But Jesus taught that God is not like this. He taught that God freely forgives the person who asks for forgiveness, without any thought of restitution or an atoning offering. The father of the Prodigal Son welcomed back his repentant son simply because the son had returned and repented, without any thought of restitution of the fortune the son had squandered. Lk 15, 11-32. In the parable of the Unforgiving Servant, the king freely canceled the debt of the supplicant debtor. Mt 18, 23-35. In the parable of the Pharisee and the Publican, the publican prayed, "God, be merciful to me, a sinner," and he, not the Pharisee, was immediately justified. Lk 18, 10-14. But the God of Anselm's explanation is not able to forgive without an acceptable atoning offering. Anselm's explanation rejects Jesus's own teachings about God and about the gratuitous availability of God's forgiveness to those who ask for it.

Fifth, central to Anselm's explanation is the assumption that the proper human response to God's anger, the proper human appeal to God's justice, and the proper human satisfaction for the sins of mankind is a human sacrifice.

First let us be clear on the terminology. By "sacrifice" I mean the ritual ceremony in which a community, in the firm belief that it will be pleasing to their god, selects a representative victim, a scapegoat, and kills the victim. Think of the Aztecs: the priests, the virginal victims, the processions, the glistening knives, the flowing blood. The Israelites believed in and practiced sacrifice in this way, although they substituted a bull or a goat for the human victim. See Leviticus 16. But the word "sacrifice" is sometimes used to describe something entirely different, which is better called "self-sacrifice." This is the altruistic act of a person who is willing to put himself or herself in harm's way to save the life of another or to remain steadfast to his or her own principles. As a familiar example of the former, think of the soldier in the foxhole who falls on the hand grenade to save the lives of his buddies, or the firefighters who ran up the stairs of the burning World Trade Center towers just before the buildings collapsed. As an example of the latter, think of the Christian martyrs who refused to worship idols, or of John McCain in the North Vietnam prison when he refused to sign a "confession" of his "crimes." Jesus's death was certainly a self-sacrifice in this sense. But in Anselm's explanation, it is sacrifice in the first sense that is meant.

Where did this strange notion that God would be pleased with the murder of a sacrificial victim come from? I will discuss the origins of sacrifice in Chapter III. For the moment, it is sufficient to say that from the most ancient times, human sacrifice had always been the center of all pagan religions. It was how humans had always placated their gods. Perhaps because the Jews had for ages worshiped the one true God with blood sacrifices and burnt offerings, Christian theologians seem to have accepted without critical examination the idea that God demanded a human sacrifice, and was pleased with it. For example, Thomas Aquinas speaks of the "satisfaction of Christ" this way:

> "A proper satisfaction comes about when someone offers to the person offended *something which gives him a delight greater than his hatred of the offense.* Now Christ by suffering as a result of love and obedience offered to God something greater than what might be exacted in compensation for the whole offense of humanity."[9]

So, according to Thomas Aquinas, God took delight in the suffering and death of Jesus! This is not the true God; this is a primitive pagan construct of a god. We cannot reconcile such a god with the Father of whom Jesus said, "If you, then, who are evil, know how to give your children what is good, how much more will your Father in heaven give good things to those who ask him!" Mt 7, 11. Jesus also said, "Go and learn the meaning of the words, 'What I want is mercy, not sacrifice.'" Mt 9, 13. The notion that God would find delight and satisfaction in the suffering and death of his only Son is truly repugnant and profoundly pagan, and has no place in Christianity.

Sixth, Anselm's explanation depends on a schizophrenic and self-destructive division in the mind of God. As the American Evangelical theologian Donald Bloesch expresses the doctrine of atonement, "The deepest meaning of the cross is not that God's wrath was poured out on a perfect or innocent man, a scapegoat for human sin, but that *God turned his wrath upon himself* in the person of his Son."[10] This is a truly schizophrenic God. But it cannot be so. God is one. God cannot be both angry and vengeful in one person, and loving and self-sacrificing in another person, at the same time. That is simply two different Gods. God cannot be angry and vengeful at one time, and loving and self-sacrificing at another time, because God is eternal, and he does not change. If God was ever wrathful, he is always and eternally wrathful. If, as Jesus taught, God is loving and caring, he is always, and eternally, loving and caring.

Christianity, like Judaism and Islam, is a strictly monotheistic religion. There is one perfect, omnipotent, eternal and unchanging God. The simultaneously wrathful and merciful God of Anselm's explanation is not the Christian God. It is the apotheosis of the familiar human story of a stubborn and prideful old man arguing with a son who sees things in a different light.

Seventh, Anselm's explanation makes humanity a wholly passive beneficiary of its own redemption. (This is also a problem with both the deliverance theory and the demonstration theory of Jesus's mission referred to above.) The decisive atoning act is an arrangement between God the Father and God the Son. Humanity plays no part except to kill Jesus. There is nothing humans can do to appease God's wrath or to bridge the gap between God and man. So the redemption of humanity is concluded without any meaningful participation by men or women. It is argued that humanity participated because Jesus was a man. Here we have one more unelected "representative," one more indefensible legal fiction. But even though Jesus was human, his sacrifice was effective, according to the theory, only because he was God the Son. His humanity had no effect on the quality of his sacrifice. In any event, according to Anselm's explanation, Jesus alone arranged the atonement and achieved the redemption. The rest of us have no participation, except to choose to enjoy the benefits of redemption by accepting Jesus as our redeemer.

Eighth, the crucifixion, in Anselm's explanation, involves yet another transfer of responsibility, blame and liability for punishment for sin. Jesus himself was sinless, and had nothing to atone for. Anselm's theory seeks to overcome this problem by asserting that Jesus "took on" the sins of all of humanity. But each person is responsible for his own sins and no person is responsible for the sins of others (except to the extent that his or her own evil actions have induced others to sin). Responsibility for one's own life and for one's own conduct is not transferable. One cannot "take on" another's sins. If Jesus had "died for our sins," he would have suffered evil, but the sins would still be our sins. As we shall see in Chapter III, humans can persuade themselves that they have transferred their sins and the responsibility for their own evil actions to a victim, and they have frequently done so. This is the essence of the pagan sacrifice. But this is always self-deception, and a lie. This profoundly pagan lie is at the foundation of the doctrine of "substitutionary atonement." Thomas Cahill concurs with these conclusions when he says,

> "We do not have to adopt a theory of substitution—the theory that God required a spotless human victim to make up for human sin—to make sense of the Crucifixion. Such

a theory, it seems to me, is a remnant of prehistoric paganism and its beliefs in cruel divinities who demanded blood sacrifice."[11]

Ninth, in Anselm's explanation, the death of Jesus, as a perfect sacrifice to the Father, is the effective redeeming act. As the ballad puts it, "Jesus our Savior did come for to die." As the English Evangelical theologian John R. W. Stott expressed it, "The mission of a lifetime of thirty to thirty-five years was to be accomplished in its last twenty-four hours, indeed, its last six."[12] This makes the teachings of Jesus at best incidental and at worst irrelevant to his mission. (This may explain in part why many Christians don't pay much attention to them.) If Anselm's explanation is correct, teaching and working miracles must have been just Jesus's way of passing the time while he awaited his death. Their only relationship to his redeeming act was to make the leaders of the Jews sufficiently hostile to him that they would accomplish his death.

But as I said at the outset, if we want to know why Jesus came, we should look at what he said. In fact, he repeatedly expressed a quite contrary view. As I will show in Chapter V, Jesus himself repeatedly said that his teaching was what he came to do, and that salvation would come from his teaching.

I conclude, then, that Anselm's explanation, and the traditional teaching of the Christian Churches which it sets forth, is fatally flawed in every particular.

Criticisms From Other Writers.

I am certainly not the first person to have seen these flaws in Anselm's explanation. Most Christians understand that the story of Adam and Eve is a primitive myth. Most people, if they think about it, will agree that the idea of the inheritability of sin, guilt and liability for punishment is an unjust and pernicious concept.

The general view of Christians toward the idea of a wrathful God who demands sacrifice is more complex. Old Testament imagery is so firmly embedded in both Catholic and Protestant

Christian teaching that many people accept the notion of an angry and wrathful God. At the same time, the same people pray to the same God as the God of loving kindness and infinite forgiveness described by Jesus. And most people set aside as insoluble the problem of reconciling the contradictions between these two views. How a loving and merciful God could have taken delight in the murder of his own Son is such a difficult thing to grasp that most of us have simply considered it a mystery and have left it alone. The time has come for us to recognize that this is an irreconcilable conflict, and that we must choose one over the other. I trust that you, like me, will choose the God of loving kindness of whom Jesus spoke. Similarly, most Christians accept the teaching that the crucifixion of Jesus was his essential redeeming act, even though this means that both his teaching and his resurrection are marginalized. This is also a contradiction we cannot continue to accept.

A number of contemporary Christian writers working in quite different problem areas have severely criticized Anselm's explanation and the doctrine of substitutionary atonement. James Carroll's *Constantine's Sword*[13] is a history of Christian persecution of the Jews. In the middle of his book, Carroll devotes a chapter to the faults of Anselm's explanation.[14] He argues that because Anselm's theory makes the crucifixion of Jesus his central redeeming act and the center of his mission, it has caused undue emphasis to be placed on the question of who killed Jesus, and has justified the actions of the Christian Churches in blaming the Jews. He calls for a new Vatican Council for the Roman Catholic Church, and proposes that such a council adopt a new Christology free from Anselm's explanation and its anti-Semitic overtones.[15] But Carroll does not himself propose a coherent developed theory of Jesus's mission to replace Anselm's explanation.

Proverbs of Ashes, by Rita Nakashima Brock and Rebecca Ann Parker,[16] is an indictment of Anselm's (and Calvin's) explanation by two American Protestant theologians. They argue, and attest quite movingly from personal experience, that because of Anselm's explanation, Christian women have been taught to accept and bear domestic violence and sexual abuse as Jesus accepted and bore the cross. Anselm's explanation is in their view profoundly sexist and anti-feminist. Rita Nakashima Brock writes:

> "At the center of western Christianity is the story of the cross, which claims God the Father required the death of his Son to save the world. We believe this theological claim sanctions violence. We seek a different theological vision."[17]

And Rebecca Ann Parker writes:

> "Christian theology presents Jesus as the model of self-sacrificing love and persuades us [women] to believe that sexism is divinely sanctioned. We are tied to the virtue of self-sacrifice, often by hidden social threats of punishment. We keep silent about rape, we deny when we are being abused, and we allow our lives to be consumed by the trivial and by our preoccupation with others. . . . The Bible suggests that sexism marks the fall of humanity. Exiled from the Garden of Eden, Adam and Eve are cursed with the loss of mutuality. Women will experience their sexuality as a source of pain, and men will lord it over them (Genesis 3: 16). Primordial estrangement from God is manifest in social systems of dominance and submission. . . . The dynamic of dominance and submission in human relations is the heart of sin."[18]

But neither Rita Brock nor Rebecca Parker proposes a coherent alternative explanation for the mission of Jesus.

René Girard has written a series of books about the place of violence, sacrifice and the sacred in the cultural development of humanity.[19] I will discuss some of his findings and theories in Chapter III. Girard has this to say about Anselm's explanation:

"It must be admitted that nothing in what the Gospels tell us directly about God justifies the inevitable conclusion of a sacrificial reading of the Epistle to the Hebrews. This conclusion was most completely formulated by the medieval theologians, and it amounts to the statement that the Father himself insisted upon the sacrifice. Efforts to explain this sacrificial pact only result in absurdities: God feels the need to revenge his honor, which has been tainted by the sins of humanity, and so on. Not only does God require a new victim, but he requires the victim who is most precious and most dear to him, his very son. No doubt this line of reasoning has done more than anything else to discredit Christianity in the eyes of people of goodwill in the modern world. However acceptable to the medieval mind it might have been, it has become intolerable for us, and it forms the major stumbling-block for a world that is entirely (and quite justifiably) hostile to the idea of sacrifice, even though that hostility remains tinged with sacrificial elements which no one has succeeded in rooting out."[20]

Girard's writings contain the basis for part of my alternative explanation for the mission of Jesus. I will incorporate many of his insights into the theory advanced in this book. But he has not undertaken to set forth his own explanation of the mission of Jesus in a work addressing that matter directly.

The Canadian Presbyterian theologian Douglas John Hall carries this argument to its natural conclusion: that is, that Anselm's explanation *cannot* be believed:

"We have noted that by far the most influential atonement theology of Western Christendom hinges upon the concept of sacrificial substitution: Jesus, the pure and innocent Lamb of God, accepts in his own person the just judgment of God, thus propitiating for 'the sins of the whole world'; if we believe this and avail ourselves of the ritual and other means of grace, we may be saved from the divine wrath and become recipients of eternal life.

"But 'we' do not believe this. Some in our midst do believe it, or say they do, and we are not permitted to discredit the sincerity of their claim; but *the vast majority of those who will read these words not only do not but probably cannot believe this, or even comprehend profoundly what believing it entails.* For the theory is impossibly interwoven with medieval feudal and even superstitious practices and folklore, to say nothing of its unworthy representation of the biblical God to whom sacrifice was made.

"In other words, the most powerful and (so far as Western Christendom is concerned) almost exclusive doctrinal tradition concerning Christ's priestly work seems fundamentally inaccessible to us."[21]

As the old saw goes, "You can't fight something with nothing." Anselm's explanation has persisted through nine centuries in part because it is the only comprehensive explanation of the mission of Jesus to have been set forth in the last millennium. James Carroll calls it the "default" theory of Christianity.[22] I take him to mean that whatever the weaknesses of Anselm's explanation, it will survive until a different and plausible comprehensive explanation of the mission of Jesus comes forward.

I propose a wholly different and comprehensive explanation of Jesus's mission, an entirely different answer to the question why God became man. I continue to hold the core Christian assertion that God redeemed humanity through Jesus, and through Jesus alone, and that Jesus's mission was thus the redemption of humanity. But I propose a wholly different understanding of the meaning of this redemption.

The redemption of humanity presupposes two things: first, that in some way humanity needs a redemption, needs a divine intervention to achieve some goal or destiny; and second, that the situation of humanity is such that a redemption can take place. In the absence of the story of the Fall of Adam and Eve, we need to discover first what in the situation of humanity needed the redemptive intervention of Jesus, and second what in the situation of humanity will make Jesus's redemptive activity effective. I propose to do this in the next several chapters.

Is this a book, then, about the accuracy of a relatively obscure eleventh-century theological dialogue? Most emphatically not! It is not a good thing to have a theory, Anselm's explanation, at the center of our understanding of Jesus, when the theory has all the faults and flaws pointed out above. It is far worse to have such a theory obscure and disguise the true mission of Jesus, which is what it does. Anselm's explanation is a tangle of briars and brambles obscuring the path. When we clear the path, we can approach an understanding of what Jesus really intended. Jesus called us to follow him. How can we follow him until we can see where he is going? Jesus's teaching, placed in context and thoughtfully studied, shows where he was going, what he was doing and how he wanted us to follow him. If we see this, we will see Christianity in a new, different and clearer light. We will be able to understand for the first time since the days of the earliest Christians what it means to be a Christian, to be a follower of Jesus. We will in this light be able to see what must be changed in the current practice of the Christian Churches and of the Christian life. This is far from an eleventh-century problem.

Notes:
1. Hall, Douglas John, *Professing the Faith* (Fortress Press, 1993), pp. 403, 416-33.
2. *Ibid.*, p. 424.
3. See, *e.g.*, McGrath, Alister E., *Christian Theology, An Introduction, 3d Ed.* (Blackwell Publishers, 2001), pp. 419-21.
4. Brock, Rita Nakashima and Parker, Rebecca Ann, *Proverbs of Ashes* (Beacon Press, 2001), p. 29.
5. *Catechism of the Catholic Church* (Doubleday Image Books, 1995), Sections 613-14.

6. Eibl-Eibesfeldt, Irenaus, *The Biology of Peace and War* (Viking Press, 1979), pp. 125-29.

7. *Ibid.*, pp. 129-40.

8. Meyr, Ernst, *What Evolution Is* (Basic Books, 2001), pp. 81-82.

9. Aquinas, Thomas, *Summa Theologiae*, IIIa, q.48, a.2, quoted in McGrath, *op. cit.*, pp. 420-21 (Emphasis added).

10. Bloesch, Donald G., *Essentials of Evangelical Theology, Vol 1* (Harper-Collins, 1982), p. 161 (Emphasis added).

11. Cahill, Thomas, *Desire of the Everlasting Hills* (Talese/Anchor Books, 2001), p. 293.

12. Stott, John R. W., *The Cross of Christ* (InterVarsity Press, 1986), p. 67.

13. Carroll, James, *Constantine's Sword* (Houghton Mifflin, 2001).

14. *Ibid.*, pp. 278-89.

15. *Ibid.*, pp. 577-87.

16. Brock and Parker, *op. cit.*

17. *Ibid.*, p. 8.

18. *Ibid.*, pp. 36-37.

19. Girard, René, *Violence and the Sacred* (Johns Hopkins University Press, 1977); *Things Hidden Since the Foundation of the World* (Stanford University Press, 1987); *The Scapegoat* (Johns Hopkins University Press, 1986).

20. Girard, René, *Things Hidden Since the Foundation of the World* (Stanford University Press, 1987), p. 182.

21. Hall, *op. cit.*, pp. 500-01 (Emphasis added).

22. Carroll, *op. cit.*, p. 298.

II

THE BEHAVIORS OF NATURAL SELECTION.

I would like to describe my explanation of the mission of Jesus to you as it came to me, so you could follow with me my path of discovery. Unfortunately for this approach, I developed my explanation backwards. I began with the conviction that Jesus's death was not an atoning sacrifice to a wrathful God. I then analyzed the teachings of Jesus to see whether they showed what he thought he had come to do. At the same time I studied the writings of René Gerard, describing the fundamentally violent nature of all human sacrificial religions and the anti-sacrificial meaning of Jesus's death. I began to understand the direct and thorough opposition of the teachings of Jesus to the foundations of the culture of the ancient civilizations built upon religions of sacrifice. Only later did I discover the development by evolutionary psychologists within the last thirty years or so of an understanding of the behaviors of humans which are embedded in the human genome by natural selection. This discovery is the last piece of the theory, but it is the place where an orderly explanation must start.

The universal conviction of Christians is that in some way Jesus redeemed mankind. We believe that his redemption works a moral and spiritual change in humans and in the relationship of humans with God. But what needed to be changed? What was the relationship of humans with God, and why did it need changing? We need to examine the moral and spiritual characteristics, the moral strengths and weaknesses, of humanity as it existed prior to the change effected by Jesus's redemption of humanity, to understand what in humans was or is to be changed, or redeemed, and how.

Moral attributes of humans, like all our other behavioral attributes, are partially genetic and partially cultural—part nature, part nurture. Our genetic inheritance precedes all human culture, so it seems to me that the proper place to begin is with the behavioral attributes which are part of our genetic heritage.

Our genes are what they are because of the evolution of humanity (along with all other forms of life) from a common ancestor by natural selection. The principles of evolution by natural selection, substantially set forth by Charles Darwin in *The Origin of Species* in 1859, are the central principles of modern biology. I accept the principles of evolution by natural selection, as I accept the movement of the planets around the sun, not just as scientific truth, but as truth. Similarly, I accept the resurrection of Jesus not just a religious truth, but as truth. Let me say a bit about how I have personally worked out the relationship between science, in this case biology, and religion. I firmly believe that truth is one. Truth is discovered by the natural operation of human intelligence. I hold that truth in matters of religion is learned and known by the inquiring human mind in the same way as truth in matters of science, although each has its own distinctive way of proceeding to find the truth. So I firmly believe that one cannot hold religious views which are irreconcilably inconsistent with one's scientific views.

The overwhelming evidence developed by scientists over the last two centuries has demonstrated that the evolution of mankind from animals by natural selection is established fact, just as the movement of the planets around the sun is established fact. Religious views to the contrary simply cannot be maintained. But I do not simply maintain that theology must reconcile itself to scientific truth. I believe that the findings of scientists, at this point in evolutionary psychology, and at a later point in cultural anthropology, provide an important basis for theological insights which could not be reached without them.

Natural Selection.

The fundamental principles of evolution by natural selection are these. No two individuals of a population are exactly the same. No two individuals have exactly the same genes. Some of the differences between individuals arise from the differences in their genes. Some of these differences affect the probability that a given individual will survive and reproduce. The next succeeding generation will not receive a recombination of the genes of the previous generation in the same proportions in which they occurred in the previous generation; it will receive a recombination of the genes of those individuals of the previous generation which survived and successfully reproduced. Over a long period of time, those genes which have enhanced the probability that the individual carrying them will reproduce, will increase in frequency in the population. Genes having the same function, but which do not enhance the probability that their carrier will reproduce, will die out. This is the essence of natural selection.[1]

A contemporary example of natural selection is the evolution of antibiotic-resistant bacteria. In a large colony of bacteria, a very few bacteria will be resistant to antibiotics. As long as no antibiotics are present, this characteristic gives no reproductive advantage, and the resistant bacteria will continue to be few. Antibiotics work to cure a bacterial infection, because they kill most of the infecting bacteria in the patient. With the introduction of antibiotics to the bacteria's environment, antibiotic-resistant bacteria have a huge reproductive advantage. Fewer bacteria which are not antibiotic-resistant will survive to the reproductive stage and succeed in reproducing; more of the resistant bacteria will do so. With each generation, the proportion of antibiotic-resistant bacteria in the colony will increase. After many generations, all the surviving and reproducing bacteria in the colony will be antibiotic-resistant. This is how natural selection works.

Natural selection is a wholly automatic process. It occurs

whenever there is genetic variability within a population and competition for survival and reproductive opportunity. It is unguided, and as amoral as the rain or the tides. It is generally very slow. Thousands or millions of generations may be needed to establish an evolutionary change in the genome by natural selection. Many of the genetic attributes of humans, including the behavioral attributes we shall discuss in this chapter, evolved by natural selection to maximize human survival and reproduction in the environment in which that evolution took place, which was for a very long time the environment of small tribes of prehominids on the bush savannas of Africa. Bacteria also evolve slowly over many thousands of generations, but because bacteria produce new generations so quickly, they evolve over a much shorter time period. This is how bacteria have evolved antibiotic-resistant strains in just a few decades.

A few caveats and distinctions: First, some behavioral inclinations of humans are found in our genes, placed there by natural selection. Other behaviors are culturally-based behaviors, and human culture also changes over time, or evolves (in a non-biological sense). Cultural evolution changes human life and behavioral inclinations much more rapidly than natural selection, but it does not change the genes. So we have not evolved a genetic fitness to drive cars or to watch the news on CNN. Second, natural selection, having selected a genetic adaptation which enhances fitness to survive and reproduce in a particular environment, does not as a rule eliminate that adaptation when it is no longer needed or desirable. We all still have appendixes, although they perform no useful function. If humans had been designed from scratch to walk on two legs, instead of being incrementally adapted from four-legged ancestors, people would not so frequently suffer from back trouble. As back trouble does not ordinarily affect one's fitness to survive and reproduce, it has not been subject to alleviation or elimination by natural selection.

Human Genetically-Based Behavior.

The human *tabula* was never *rasa*. All humans are born with built-in behavior patterns. The relatively new science of Darwinian anthropology, or evolutionary psychology, which has developed in the last forty years or so, is a study of genetically-based human behavior patterns which influence human moral conduct.[2]

Evolutionary psychology does not study the biological basis of all human activity. It is not concerned with our evolved behavior in using our hands to carry food to the mouth, or our similarities to the chimpanzees in the act of peeling a banana. Instead, evolutionary psychology has concentrated on the evolutionary basis of certain anti-social behavioral characteristics or tendencies of all humans which make human life more difficult. These are violence against other humans, acquisitiveness and greed, kinship loyalty combined with fear and hatred of strangers, and dominant-submissive patterns of conduct.[3] Some evolutionary psychologists have concentrated their studies on genetically-based violence, including rape, murder, war and genocide.[4] Others have given more attention to kinship selection.[5] I shall treat all four behaviors as of equal importance for my purposes.

Evolutionary psychologists have gone to considerable effort to establish, against the cultural behaviorists, that these behaviors are not simply cultural behaviors, but are actually found in our genes. This distinction is important, for three reasons. First, genetically-based behaviors are to be found in all humans with little variation. Such variations in these behaviors as are found are due to cultural modification. Second, genetically-based anti-social behaviors are uniform throughout all humanity through all ages, because they pass from generation to generation by procreation, and they remained unchanged unless modified by natural selection. In this respect they are as uniform and pervasive as traditional original sin, and differ from it only in that no human can or should be blamed or punished, or separated from God, on account of his or her genetic inheritance. Third, cultural behaviors can and do overlay the genetically-based behaviors, and can work with them or against them, as we choose. Cultural behaviors can pass from one generation to another only by teaching and example, and cannot pass by procreation. So in each generation we have some responsibility for and some control over our culturally-based behaviors.

For these reasons, we need to be able to distinguish genetically-based behaviors from culturally-based behaviors. So we need to follow rather closely how the genetic basis for the behaviors identified as genetic by the evolutionary psychologists has been established. There seem to be two indicators that a specific behavior is genetic. First, behavioral characteristics can find their way into our genes if and only if those behaviors have consistently conferred a reproductive advantage on those individuals who possess them, and thus could have been, and probably were, naturally selected. To show that certain behavior patterns are genetic, and not simply derived from human culture, therefore, we need to find that they conferred a reproductive advantage. Second, if we also see similar patterns of behavior in the great apes, and in other animals, that evidence confirms the conclusion that those behavior patterns evolved by natural selection and are in the human genome, because human cultural development could not have accounted for their presence in animals. Let us examine the behaviors listed above, one by one, for their possession of a reproductive advantage and for their presence in animals.

Violence. A fundamental difference between men and women, and between males and females of almost every mammal species, is the very large difference in time commitment required for a given reproductive opportunity. The male impregnates the egg of the female, and he's done. The female has just begun. She must bear the fertilized egg, then the embryo, then the fetus, to birth, and, in mammals, nurse the newborn until it is weaned. A male is most successful in getting his genes to the next generation if he mates with as many females as possible, as often as possible. From the male point of view, the lengthy time commitment required of the female for reproduction, during which she is unavailable for new reproductive activity, very severely limits the available reproductive opportunities for males. So males compete with each other for reproductive opportunity.[6] In many species, including all primates, this is a violent competition. Male gorillas regularly fight to the death to win and then preserve exclusive mating opportunities with a group of females.[7] The victor in these fights gets its genes to the next generation; the vanquished does not. The genes of the bigger, stronger, quicker, more aggressive and more violent males thus increase in frequency in the population with each generation. Natural selection thus selects for violence and aggressive behavior, particularly in males. This is why males have testosterone, and why men are generally bigger and stronger than women.

Acquisitiveness. Females generally do not need to compete with each other to get males willing to reproduce; there is an oversupply. Females can select among available males. In many animal species, females select for fitness, strength, aggression and dominance. Natural selection will reward females who select for these qualities by making it more likely that their offspring, particularly their male offspring, will have these traits and will themselves survive and successfully reproduce. But significantly, among the higher primates and humans, females will also select for signs of male parental investment, that is, indications that the male will still be around during the periods of gestation and infancy to provide protection to mother and offspring.[8]

In the prehominid period from as long as five million years ago, the size of the brain in the direct ancestors of humans increased threefold. There was no similar increase in the size of the birth canal during that period; successful live births were those that occurred ever earlier in the gestation period. The result of this evolution is that human newborns are far more helpless than newborns of other species. The importance of a male who could provide not only protection but food and shelter during this prolonged infancy period increased. Successful females selected not only for strength and fitness, but also for male parental investment and wealth, even if the wealth was nothing more than weapons for hunting and control of a place of shelter. Thus males who acquired possessions and showed their ability to get and keep them were more frequently selected by females. Possession of goods, or the desire for possessions and the willingness and ability to use violence if necessary to obtain them, was thus favored by natural selection.

Kinship Altruism. Charles Darwin delayed the publication of *The Origin of Species* for many years while he tried to solve the problem of the ant which fights to the death to defend the ant colony, or the sterile worker bee. How can natural selection favor the development of attributes which make survival or reproduction impossible? There seem to be two closely-related and overlapping answers.

First, natural selection favors altruism within a family or kinship group. If an ant or a bee has the genetic trait of willingness to fight to the death for the colony or to die without reproducing for the hive, that genetic trait will likely be found in the reproducing members of the colony or hive as well, because as kin they share the same genes. The labor or defense supplied by the non-reproducing members protects the colony or hive and thus gives a reproductive advantage to the reproducing kin of the non-reproducing members. Thus self-sacrificing genetic behavior survives. It is similar with humans. Any behavioral attribute of a parent which enhances the survival and fitness of offspring will be favored by natural selection, because such activity helps the transmission of the parents' genes to the generation of grandchildren. A parent, wishing all of its offspring to survive and reproduce, will train or teach the offspring to share with one another, not to fight with each other, and to support and care for one another. These activities will be favored by natural selection. Affection, loyalty and altruism among siblings and cousins enhance the probability of survival and reproduction for all the members of the kinship group.

Second, cooperative activity within a group will sometimes itself enhance the probability of survival and reproduction of members of the group, whether there is a blood relationship among its members or not. A group of chimpanzees or of prehominids will hunt or make war more effectively as a cooperative group than as lone individuals. It is likely that this kind of cooperative behavior originated with kinship cooperation, gradually extending to more distant kin. To the extent that cooperation among members of a group enhances the survival of its members, it will be selected by natural selection.[9]

Kinship altruism and cooperative group altruism are both a long way from altruism toward all the individuals who are members of one's species. In many important ways, kin and group altruism are opposed to universal altruism. The kinship group naturally identifies itself in contrast with and in opposition to those who are not kin. The cooperative group frequently achieved its unity in the bonding activity of war and pillage against those outside the group. The eminent biologist Ernst Mayr states this conclusion as follows:

> "The same kinds of altruism that are extended to other members of a social group are rarely offered to outsiders. Different social groups usually compete with each other and not infrequently fight each other. There is little doubt that hominid history is a history of genocide. Indeed, the same can apparently be said about chimpanzees. How then could . . . . altruism toward outsiders have become established in the human species? Could natural selection be invoked? This has often been tried, but not very successfully. It is difficult to construct a scenario in which benevolent behavior toward competitors and enemies could be rewarded by natural selection. It is interesting in this connection to read the Old Testament and see how consistently a difference is made between behavior toward one's own group and behavior to any outsiders. This is in total contrast to the ethics promoted in the New Testament. Jesus's parable of the altruism of the Good Samaritan was a striking departure from custom.

Altruism toward strangers is a behavior not supported by natural selection."[10]

Dominant-Submissive and Hierarchical Behaviors. Within many groups of animals, there have evolved behaviors in which individuals test their strength against others within the group in contests which stop short of mortal injury or death. Chimpanzee communities are closed groups within which a distinct social ranking system exists. Ranking within the community is established and maintained by fighting and by intimidation behavior which rarely results in serious injury to the combatants.[11] Natural selection favors such behaviors where they enhance survival and provide stability to the closed group (while in contrast natural selection would not favor intra-group fighting to the death). An example of hierarchical behavior in animals is found in the term "pecking order," which describes the behavior of hens. If one puts a group of hens together, there will initially be a period of instability, dispute and combat. After a time, the hens settle down into a linear hierarchy. Hen A pecks Hen B, Hen B pecks Hen C, and so on. Each hen dominates those lower than her in the hierarchy, and submits to the hens above her. Dominance-submission hierarchies are found in many mammals and in all primates, including primitive humans.[12]

Summary. Natural selection, which permitted prehominids to evolve from the great apes, and humans from the prehominids, gave the earliest humans a genetic system with some built-in genetic behavior patterns. The first humans, the ancestors of all of us, were violent. The males were highly-evolved and successful fighters, hunters and killers.[13] They desired possessions and secure territory, and were willing and able to wage war to acquire and hold them. They were loyal to and cooperative with kin and fellow members of their tribe or clan, and suspicious and fearful of, and hostile to, all others. Their tribes or communities were dominant-submissive hierarchical organizations, with chiefs, workers, and slaves. So much for the Garden of Eden, and the life of the first humans in Paradise!

It is a sobering thought to realize that the behavior patterns which were bred into the genes of the earliest humans by natural selection are still in the genetic makeup of every human now alive. Natural selection is very slow, and ten thousand generations (roughly the time span since the emergence of Homo Sapiens) is a very short time on the clock of evolution. The human genome has not changed significantly since the dawn of humanity. And even over a much longer period of time, there is no hope that the human genome will change so as to reduce or eliminate these behavioral tendencies. Natural selection will not change them. There is no reason to think that avoidance of violence, of hunger for possessions, of kinship loyalty or of dominant-submissive behavior would increase any individual's chances of survival or reproductive opportunity in a way which would cause these genetic behaviors to be selected against. Natural selection does not have the betterment of the species as a goal. Even if these behaviors, at least in their primitive forms, are in many ways obsolete or even harmful, we have retained and will retain them in our genetic material for the future, as we will still have appendixes and bad backs.

The Economy of God.

I am writing from the perspective of a Christian who believes that there is a creator God, benevolent to humans, who has a plan for the perfection of humanity. Whether a benevolent creator God exists, and why I believe one does exist, is matter for another book, not this one. Discerning and describing God's plan for humanity, as best I can, is closely related to discerning and describing the mission of Jesus, and thus is part of this book. So the question arises: How can it be part of God's plan that all humans have implanted in our genes the anti-social behavior patterns found there by the Darwinian anthropologists? I think the way to explain my approach to this question is to look in a broader way at two fundamental problems many of us have with the ways of God toward humans, God's silence and human suffering, and then return to the genetic behavior patterns of mankind.

Many people reject or resist the idea of God and the idea that God has a benevolent plan for humans because of their experience of the silence of God. Some Christians believe, and are happy to testify, that God has spoken to them, or that they have been moved by God to accept Jesus Christ as their Lord and Savior. I am happy for them, but I have never felt God speaking to me. I have prayed, but I do not have any clear experience of God answering my prayers. I have not been moved to accept Jesus as my Lord and Savior by any emotional experience. I have worked hard and reflected deeply before I reached an acceptance of Jesus. I have doubted, and no answers were delivered to me. I think many people share my experience, and have felt the silence of God. The Christian revelation, as found in scripture, was concluded shortly after the end of the first century A.D. I suppose that many of my readers, to the extent they've thought about it, have felt from time to time, or even most of the time, as I have, that if God wants me to believe something, or to do something, he knows where I am. Yet he has remained silent.

A similar and more distressing problem with God, to believing Christians as well as to those who do not believe, is the enormous amount of evil, sin and suffering in the world. We need only look at the twentieth century: the slaughter of the First World War; the horrors of the Second World War; the Holocaust; the Bomb; Korea; Vietnam; Biafra; Bosnia; Rwanda; the influenza, polio and AIDS epidemics; the earthquakes in Turkey and India, and the floods in China and Bangladesh; and, closer to home, Oklahoma City, Columbine and the World Trade Center. And now anthropological biology instructs us that it was ever thus; perennial conflict and violence was bred into the genetic makeup as well as found in the environment of the earliest humans. How could a benevolent or a perfect God permit such things?

There can be no really satisfactory answer to the problems of the silence of God and the suffering of humanity. But perhaps an approach to an explanation can be found in the modern scientific view of the world. We see in the discoveries of modern science the astonishing fact that the human mind can see deeply into the workings of the natural world, and that from this vision men and women can and have fashioned remedies or cures for many of the evils which have long plagued mankind. Albert Einstein once said that "The most incomprehensible thing about the universe is that it is comprehensible."[14] It would be insensitive to lose one's sense of wonder about this. If humans are so made as to be able to discover and comprehend the secrets of nature, this is not accidental; it is intended. God created humans to use this extraordinary capacity. God intends men and women to figure things out for themselves, and to create with their own resources their culture, their civilizations and their lives.

This general observation applies not only in science, but in nearly every field of human endeavor. Even to the believer in revealed truth, there is little or no divine revelation on how men and women should organize their civil societies. The divine right of kings does not have scriptural support. Humans have been inventing and reforming their means of governing their communities from time immemorial, by trial and error. While mankind has made some progress, there is clearly plenty of need for further invention and reformation. There is no divine revelation about how to make art or music (although I think a case can be made for believing that God spoke to us through Mozart). In art as well as in governance, we proceed by trial and error, and it often seems that for every three steps forward, we take two steps back. But that is the glory, or the curse, of mankind: we're on our own, and as a general rule, it appears that God has always intended for us to be on our own.

To me, this is the explanation for the silence of God, and for the fact that divine revelation ended with the completion of the books of the New Testament. Going forward on our own is hard work, and it requires courage as well as industry. It would be easier if God spoke to us from time to time. But nothing would so blunt the imagination and daring of determined and hard-working men and women as receiving from time to time an answer from on high. It would be our natural and unavoidable tendency to stop working and thinking hard, and await the word. If prayer, instead of work, could reliably produce prosperity or peace, we would all stop working and pray. J. K. Rowling saw that this would be true of magic. As Hagrid explained to Harry Potter:

> "But what does a Ministry of Magic do?"
> "Well, their main job is to keep it from the Muggles that there's still witches an' wizards up an' down the country."
> "Why?"
> "Why? Blimey, Harry, everyone'd be wantin' magic solutions to their problems. Nah, we're best left alone."[15]

Waiting for new revelations, or for miracles in answer to prayer, is not our destiny. To me this is why God does not usually reward the praying person with prosperity or peace (except internal peace and acceptance of one's lot). The genuine achievements and accomplishments of mankind would be very much fewer, in my view, if God were not silent.

The same answer, although harder to accept, applies to human suffering. If fire did not burn, who would learn to avoid the flames? Much human suffering through the ages has been caused by diseases which are now treatable and curable. If the diseases had not caused suffering, there would never have been the search for treatment and cure. Our destiny and our work is to think and to learn about the universe, and one goal of this learning is to use the knowledge so gained to alleviate or prevent suffering. In the last five centuries, millions of people suffered the disfiguring and often fatal curse of smallpox. Modern medicine has just about eradicated this disease from the face of the earth. The same is true for poliomyelitis. Many people are now dying of AIDS. But it is not unreasonable to expect that a vaccine or cure for HIV disease will be discovered within the next generation. In like manner, I think we now regard famine and war as preventable evils. We know how to protect homes from flooding, and how to provide clean water and sanitary sewage systems to all the people on the earth; we lack only the will to do it. And we could probably eliminate poverty from the face of the earth, if we set our minds, our wills and our resources to the task. Individual men and women still suffer, and their communities suffer, from natural and physical evils they cannot, and their communities cannot, control or alleviate. But the community of mankind can learn to control or alleviate much of this evil, and much of this suffering, as the resources of our intelligence, ingenuity, judgment and courage are brought to bear on these evils. This is part of God's plan for the destiny of humanity.

Let's return to the question with which we began: How can it be part of God's plan that all humans have implanted in our genes the anti-social behavior patterns found there by the Darwinian anthropologists? If it is true that God created humans with built-in behavior patterns of violence, fear and hatred of strangers, dominant-submissive behavior and acquisitiveness, he must have had some purpose in mind in doing so. The only alternative position is that there is no plan, and that humanity has evolved to the state it is in by a combination of accidents, coincidences and the operation of mindless natural physical laws or processes. It is difficult to find and give a coherent explanation of God's plan or purpose for humanity in general, and for humanity evolved from the lower animals with these naturally-selected anti-social tendencies in particular. As a result, many people feel that this alternative position is the only one that makes sense out of the data and out of the mixed and not very hopeful situation of humanity in this world as we know it. But I am unable to construct a meaningful and believable Christian explanation of the world which sees no divine plan in the original situation of humanity.

I suggested above that the only answer for God's silence and for human suffering which makes sense to me, if God has a plan for us at all, is that God believes that in order for humanity to grow and reach its potential, we need to be left alone to apply our intelligence and our energy to discovering the truth and to solving humanity's problems. The great social tasks of fighting disease, famine, war and poverty are tasks of all mankind. But many of us will never have the opportunity to work directly on the solutions to these evils. In contrast, the genetic inheritance of humanity, out of which much evil comes, presents a problem for the human situation with which every single person must grapple. Every man and woman must deal with his or her own inclinations toward violence, acquisitiveness, kinship loyalty and fear and hatred of strangers, and dominant-submissive behavior. In every civilized society, the early training of infants and children works to teach children to control and avoid violence, to refrain from taking what belongs to another, to have respect for and acceptance of people outside the kinship (ethnic, religious, national) group, and to treat others as equals with fairness. Our fundamental social institutions, from church groups to the criminal justice system, work toward enabling and enforcing control of our genetically-based anti-social behaviors. But each person must ultimately take responsibility for his or her own behavior, and attain as best one can a dominance of one's conscience and intellect over one's baser genetic inclinations.

If our genetic inheritance is part of God's plan for us, as I believe it is, I think it indicates that God's intention for every person is that he or she can and must develop character and strength by learning how to control his or her genetically-based behavioral tendencies. Each human becomes strong and wise only through hard work. Our genetic inheritance insures that we all have hard work to do. This is part of God's plan for the destiny of humanity.

But we are speaking here of genetically based anti-social behaviors. Human culture can increase and refine our knowledge of ourselves and of the world, and human effort and ingenuity can alleviate some of the suffering of humanity. But can human intelligence and effort resist and overcome humanity's genetic inheritance? It hasn't done so yet. We see violence, ethnic and religious hatred, wars, and concentrations of power and wealth in the few, throughout the world. From the first appearance of humans, there was a strong probability that human culture would develop (in respect of this genetic inheritance) by taking the path of lesser resistance. It would develop by channeling and controlling these genetically based behaviors and using them as the foundation blocks of the cultures of the world's great civilizations. This, I have concluded, is exactly what happened, a conclusion I will develop in the next chapter.

The creation of humanity with built-in genetically-based antisocial behaviors which (the evidence indicates) cannot be overcome by human efforts is in a very real sense an imperfect creation. And, since we have rejected the story of the Fall of Adam and Eve, and because humans can't be held responsible for the naturally-selected contents of the human genome, we can't blame the imperfection of creation on Adam and Eve, or on any humans. From this evident imperfection of creation we can draw several alternative inferences. One inference would be that God is not benevolent and loving. Another inference would be that perhaps the alternative position described above, that God had no purpose in human development at all, and that humanity is the way it is because of the operation of blind natural forces, is true. I suggest, and I believe, that there is a third alternative: God's creation of humanity was not imperfect; it was just incomplete. It was only half done. There is a second half of creation yet to come, which will complete God's creation, so that the effect of the whole is, and can be seen as, not imperfect, but the act of a benevolent and loving Creator. This second half of creation is the mission of Jesus.

Another way of expressing the same idea, this time using classical Christian terminology, is to say that the genetically-based behaviors of humanity provide for us a different way of understanding the traditional Christian doctrine of "original sin." Like classical "original sin," these behaviors are passed through natural procreation to every human being, because they are in the human genome. Like classical "original sin," these inbred behaviors, and the cultural behaviors which have been built upon them, incline men and women to individual and collective sin. Unlike classical "original sin," these behavioral inclinations themselves are not the result of any human sin or fault, and we need not and must not feel guilty or sinful or unworthy because of them. But as with classical "original sin," humanity stands in need of being redeemed from these genetically-based behaviors and the cultural behaviors based on them. We will see how Jesus's mission was a set of redemptive actions directed at this need. In this way God's plan and creative activity produced both the need for redemption and the redemption itself.

We have so far reached only the condition of the earliest humans, newly emerged from their animal predecessors. The earliest humans were a long way from what humans were and are capable of becoming. Their lives were, as Thomas Hobbes put it, "solitary, poor, nasty, brutish and short." They were also isolated from one another. In the absence of any human culture, the evolved genetic behaviors of violence and kinship loyalty would have made it impossible for human groups larger than small kinship groups to live together. Witness the situation of our nearest living relatives in the animal world, the gorillas and the chimpanzees. Gorillas live in groups no larger than one-male harems, averaging eight members.[16] Chimpanzees live in kinship groups, generally with fewer than fifty members, and make war on neighboring groups.[17] How could the earliest humans form cultural institutions to control their genetically-based behaviors if they could not gather and live peacefully in larger groups? And how could they form larger groups without first developing the necessary controlling cultural institutions? I suggest that this impasse was solved by the invention of humanity's first and oldest cultural institution, the human sacrifice. How sacrifice took root, and the consequences of its invention and development, are the subjects of the next chapter. We proceed to a discussion of the ways with which the earliest humans organized themselves and dealt with their genetic heritage.

Notes:
1. Wright, Robert, *The Moral Animal* (Vintage Books, 1994), p. 23.
2. *Ibid.*, pp. 3-7.
3. *Ibid., passim.*
4. Ghiglieri, Michael P., *The Dark Side of Man* (Perseus Books, 1999); Eibl-Eibesfeldt, Irenaus, *The Biology of Peace and War* (Viking Press, 1979).
5. Meyr, Ernst, *What Evolution Is* (Basic Books, 2001), pp. 257-60.
6. Wright, *op. cit.*, pp. 33-34.
7. Ghiglieri, *op. cit.*, pp. 130-33.
8. Wright, *op. cit.*, pp. 57-59.
9. Meyr, *op. cit.*, p. 258.
10. *Ibid.*, pp. 258-59 (Emphasis added).
11. Eibl-Eibesfeldt, *op. cit.*, pp. 63-67.
12. Wright, *op. cit.*, pp. 239-42.
13. Eibl-Eibesfeldt, *op. cit.*, pp. 125-29.
14. Quoted in Rees, Martin, *Just Six Numbers* (Basic Books, 2000), p. 10.
15. Rowling, J. K., *Harry Potter and the Philosopher's Stone* (Bloomsbury Publishing, 1997), p. 51.
16. Ghiglieri, *op. cit.*, p. 130.
17. *Ibid.*, pp. 172-76.

III

THE CULTURE OF SACRIFICE.

Anselm's explanation, and the traditional Christian doctrine it expresses, tells us that Jesus's death on the cross was a sacrifice (meaning, as I pointed out above, not an altruistic act of a self-sacrificing hero, but the ritual blood sacrifice of a human victim who actually bears the guilt for his own death). Now in the early Christian centuries people certainly knew what a sacrifice was, because sacrificial religions of all kinds (including that of Israel) were found in the Roman Empire. In Anselm's time, Northern Europe was just emerging from its pagan roots, in which sacrifice had remained the center of most religious practices. But in our day, it is very difficult or impossible for us to have any real imaginative understanding of ritual religious sacrifice. We recoil at the ritual sacrifices of the Aztecs. It is almost impossible for us to imagine that the Aztec priests, or many of them at any rate, actually thought they were doing what was good and necessary for their people as they officiated at their ceremonies and killed their victims. It is almost impossible for us to understand that, as a matter of course, priests and people really believed that the sacrificial victim was guilty of the disorder and social evil the ritual sacrifice was intended to avert. It is perhaps because we cannot really understand sacrifice that Douglas John Hall asserts that nearly all of us, even those who profess it to be true, do not and probably cannot really believe that Jesus's death was an atoning sacrifice. But sacrifice is at the root of all the ancient religions of man, and we must try to understand it, and how it "works," both from the inside and from the outside.

Sacrifice is an indescribably ancient institution, and it was universal in ancient and primitive religious practices. Sigmund Freud described its antiquity in his *Totem and Taboo* this way: "Robertson Smith explains that the sacrifice at the altar was *the essential feature* in the ritual of ancient religions. It plays the same part in all religions, so that its origin must be traced back to very general causes, operating everywhere in the same manner."[1] But how did it arise? And how did it take hold, and root itself so deeply in the ancient religions of humanity? It is not in our genetic inheritance. It is hard to think of anything less likely to be favored by natural selection than human sacrifice. It is a cultural institution.

The Origin of Sacrifice.

It is difficult to imagine how the institution of sacrifice began. We can imagine a primitive tribe in distress, praying to whatever gods may be to save them. But when we ourselves are in distress, the last thing in the world we would think of is to select one of our neighbors, or, more likely, go down to the bus station and select a stranger in town, and kill him or her in a formal ritual. Yet this is what ancient humans did all over the world. It is not an answer to say that they believed that the gods desired or demanded sacrifice. That just leaves us with the same question: how in the world did ancient humans ever invent a belief in gods who desired human sacrifice? In fact, as we shall see, the sacrifice preceded the gods which (later) demanded sacrifices.

And how does sacrifice work? Ancient humans would not have so universally and for so long made human sacrifice the center of their religious rituals and myths, and made religious rituals and myths the center of their cultures, unless sacrifice really worked to change, to strengthen and to bind the people in some meaningful way. But it is difficult to see how this could be so.

The French scholar René Girard has advanced a hypothesis

which explains the mechanism of human sacrifice and its centrality in ancient and primitive civilizations.[2] I find his explanations persuasive and illuminating, and I know of no other theory which so well accounts for the origin of sacrifice. The clearest way to explain Girard's theory is to set forth a scenario in which sacrifice originates.

Let us imagine a typical tribe of the earliest humans. As must have frequently happened, two young males start a fight over a woman, or over a prize of some kind which both desire. The fighting escalates, and more young males become involved; one combatant is killed, and vengeance is required; a blood feud starts. Each act of violence produces a responding act of reciprocal violence, and soon the whole community is involved. The survival of the community is threatened because there is no way to stop the violence.

But this time, in this tribe, the creative imagination of the elders produced a solution. The growing hatred, violence and reciprocal vengeance within the community could not be stopped, but it could be channeled from the hatred of all against all to the hatred of all against one, preferably an outsider, a "scapegoat." The elders find a victim, an outsider or a cripple, and identify him or her as the source of the problems. Eager to hear this, the tribe unites against the chosen one, focusing their anger and violence, and they kill the victim. The sacrifice of the victim ends the cycle of vengeful violence within the tribe, because the community is now united in guilt and horror at their collective crime, and yet relieved that no one will seek vengeance for the death of the sacrificial victim. The community is temporarily at peace. The violence within the tribe will break out again. But when it does, the elders of the tribe know what to do. Another victim will be selected, another human sacrifice will be performed, and this time it will be performed in ritual fashion. This is the origin of sacrifice.

The people of the tribe, seeking to avoid guilt for their collective murder of an innocent victim, develop a simple and very human excuse for their crime. They transfer to the victim both the blame for the initial violence and disorder, and the credit for its surcease. This critically important transfer exonerates the people of the tribe. It also makes the victim a sacred being, because the victim has by his or her death brought peace to the tribe. The elders who officiated at the ritual sacrifice of the sacred victim have now become priests, intermediating between the people and the sacred victim, and in the name of the sacred victim they proclaim the first prohibitions and taboos. Since a frequent cause of the outbreak of male aggression and violence which started the whole problem would naturally be fighting over women, the first prohibitions were usually those against murder and incest. The taboo against murder is self-explanatory. The taboo against incest has nothing to do with interbreeding, genetics or the Oedipus complex. It was intended to prohibit sex within the immediate family simply to prevent males from fighting over the women in the family and killing their own fathers, brothers or sons.

The community has now transferred to the sacred victim, and to the sacred "god" which the victim now represents, the blame and the credit for the sacrifice which has united the community and has saved it from its own self-destructive violence. The victim is now regarded as the one who originated the sacrifice. So the community now describes its "god" as a god who requires and demands sacrifice. This description is then embodied in the ritual of the tribe, and preserved in the community's founding myth, in which the victim of the first sacrifice is transmuted into the god itself, who by his or her death creates the community. So the practice of human sacrifice, which is now a religious act, involves two real psychological transferences: first, responsibility for the violence and for the sacrificial murder is transferred from the community to the victim; and second, responsibility for requiring the sacrificial murder is transferred from the sacred victim to the god the victim has become.

It is critical to the efficacy of the sacrifice that the transference of guilt and blame from the community to the victim actually occur. As Girard describes it,

"The community satisfies its rage against an arbitrary victim in the unshakable conviction that it has found the one and only cause of its trouble. It then finds itself without adversaries, purged of all hostility against those for whom, a second before, it had shown the most extreme rage."[3]

This is a lie, an act of communal self-deception. It is the primal lie. But it was not seen as such. It is hard for modern people to see how complete the psychological transference of guilt to the victim was. But consider the white men who took part in the lynching of African Americans in the South in the late nineteenth and early twentieth centuries. They really believed that they were doing the right thing, and that all the blame and all the guilt were properly placed on the lynched victim. And consider that nearly all the Israelis firmly believe that the blame and guilt for the suffering they inflict is entirely that of the Palestinians, while nearly all the Palestinians are equally convinced that the fault, the blame and the guilt is entirely that of the Israelis.

The Culture of Sacrifice.

What comes out of this primal sacrifice and its regularly repeated ritual reenactment? What had previously been a tribe with only the cohesion of kinship and common experience now has rules of conduct and universal ethical prohibitions against murder, incest, stealing and so forth. It now has rituals with painstakingly detailed rubrics, which are important because the primal sacrifice must be exactly reproduced to have its effect. It now has a class of priests, who celebrate the ritual sacrifice and who observe specified rituals of diet, dress and cleanness to set themselves apart and maintain their ritual purity. It now has something other than blood to bind and unite the community and set it apart from and superior to their neighbors: a religion. (The root of the word "religion" is the Latin *religio*, which means "to bind.") In short, there is now a community with a human culture, which I call the "culture of sacrifice."

The culture of sacrifice "worked" for the earliest humans

because it provided what was most necessary for humanity to begin human culture: a mechanism which brought the otherwise anti-social genetic behavior patterns of humans under social control. The primary purpose and effect of the sacrifice itself was to arrest, control, and sublimate the violence of the members of the tribe, particularly the young males. The rituals, observances and taboos of the primitive sacrificial religion provided a unifying bond within the community which superseded that of blood kinship, and involved all the members of the community in the ritual practices in an active way. This gave the community the ability to increase in size beyond that of a kinship group, a great advantage in the perpetual warfare among neighboring tribes. (This would account for the fact that the culture of sacrifice is virtually universal in ancient and primitive cultures. The tribes and peoples which did not invent or discover their own sacrificial religion would have been defeated in battle by the larger and stronger communities which had developed the culture of sacrifice.)

Sacrificial communities necessarily acquired a class or caste of priests, along with a class of warriors, which gave them a hierarchical society of dominant and submissive classes, with women subjected to men, and with workers and slaves at the bottom. The patriarchal priest and warrior hierarchies naturally succeeded in concentrating the possessions and wealth of the communities in the top classes. Some hierarchies hardened into caste systems, where every individual stayed for his or her lifetime in the caste to which he or she was born, as in India. Other hierarchical societies were more flexible, and allowed young men from lower classes with intellectual or political abilities to join the priestly class, or those with athletic abilities to join the warrior class, as in early medieval Europe.

The genius of the culture of sacrifice is that it did not oppose the naturally-selected genetic behaviors of humans. It channeled them. Violence against members of the community was forbidden, but the sacrifice itself was violent, and warfare against strangers under the leadership of the hierarchy was encouraged and praised. Kinship altruism was broadened to include all those who worshiped and sacrificed together, but suspicion, fear and hatred of strangers, and warfare against them, was approved. Dominant-submissive behavior was not just permitted but required within the established hierarchy, as was concentration of wealth and power.

Because the culture of sacrifice did not resist the evolved genetic behavior patterns of humans, but instead reinforced them with sacrificial rituals, myths and rules of conduct, it has sunk deep roots into human psychology and human culture, and has the strength of biologically evolved and culturally developed behaviors combined. The culture of sacrifice has what the anthropological biologists call evolutionary stability: it is very highly resistant to change.[4] It is said of India that while India has often been conquered, its ancient culture has always absorbed the conqueror's culture and continued with little change. So the culture of sacrifice has the power to absorb and neutralize efforts to change it, and it has done so for thousands of years. I will return to this idea in Chapter VIII, where we shall see how the culture of sacrifice absorbed and neutralized much of the Christian revelation. For the moment it is enough simply to observe that we all now see violence among men, warfare or persecution between ethnic or religious groups, concentrations of wealth, and hierarchies of priests, mullahs and military leaders, in the news of the world every day. The culture of sacrifice has remained the world's dominant cultural institution.

The Sacrifice in Mythology.

The primitive ritual and sacrifice underlying the developed civilizations of antiquity is indescribably ancient. We have access to it principally by deciphering myths which shed light on practices which are otherwise lost in prehistory. Myths and rituals of tribes which remained primitive until modern times, such as those of the American Indians or the natives of Polynesia, provide some less ancient confirmation.

The oldest works of literature of every culture are its ancient myths, particularly its creation myths. In a great many of these creation myths, the creation of the world as it presently exists began with the killing of a god-like person: the first sacrificial victim. In some of the myths, the killing is suppressed, and in others the blame is already transferred to the gods, but the originating sacrifice is there. A thorough presentation of the mythological support for the origin of the culture of sacrifice I have described above is beyond the scope of this book, but some examples of creation myths from disparate sources will illustrate the kind of evidence the myths provide.

From the tales of the Montagnais Indians of eastern Quebec, Joseph Campbell tells the Legend of the North Star:

> "People of another (earlier) world were living in a village. They knew a new world was going to be formed. One day a number of them started to quarrel. One of the number was North Star. The others fell on him, meaning to kill him, but he fled and soared into the sky. All started after, but when they saw they could not get him: 'Well,' they said, 'let him be! He is North Star. He will be of use to the people of the world that is to come, as a guide by night to their travels.'"[5]

In this brief tale we see all the elements of the primeval sacrifice. There was violence among the villagers. The violence is focused on one scapegoat, North Star. He is certainly killed, but the story disguises the murder. He was probably driven off a cliff (he "soared into the sky"), a common form of sacrificial execution, because it is an ancient way of collective murder, like stoning, in which all participate and no one singly inflicts the death blow. The victim is now a sacred being, and from this time a new world is formed.

From West Ceram, in Indonesia, Campbell relates the story of Hainuwele. Hainuwele was born magically from the blood of a man which was spilled on a leaf of the first coconut palm. She produced great riches from her excrement. At the ceremonial dance of the first nine families of mankind, she gave such valuable presents to all the families that they became jealous, and they decided to kill her. On the ninth night of the festival, they drove her into a deep hole and buried her alive. Her grief-stricken father dug up and reburied parts of her body. From her body parts there grew the tuberous roots which were thereafter the principal food of the people. The goddess Satene appeared, cursed the nine families of mankind for their crime, and turned a number of their people into animals, the first animals to appear on the earth. The goddess then announced that she would leave the earth forever, and that men and women could thereafter come to her only after death.[6]

In this story, we see the original collective murder of one victim, an attempt to transfer blame to the sacrificial victim, the coming of death into the world by way of this sacrifice, the deification of the victim, the origin of plant foods from the sacrificed one, the departure of the gods, and the creation of life on earth as we know it.

In ancient India, one of the most famous hymns of the Rig Veda is the Purusha Sukta, or Hymn of Man:

> "The sacrificial victim, namely, Purusha, born at the very beginning, they sprinkled with sacred water upon the sacrificial grass. With him as oblation the gods performed the sacrifice, and also the Sadhyas [a class of semidivine beings] and the rishis [ancient seers]. From that wholly offered sacrificial oblation were born the verses and the sacred chants; from it were born the meters; the sacrificial formula was born from it. From it horses were born and also those animals who have double rows of teeth; cows were born from it, and from it were born goats and sheep. When they divided Purusha, in how many different portions did they arrange him? . . . His mouth became the brahman [the priests]; his two arms were made into the rajanya [the warriors]; his two thighs the vaishyas [the merchants]; from his two feet the shudra [the serf class] was born. The moon was born from the mind, from the eye the sun was born; from the mouth Indra and Agni,

from the breath the wind was born. From the navel was the atmosphere created, from the head the heaven issued forth; from the two feet was born the earth and the quarters [of the compass] from the ear. Thus did they fashion the worlds."[7]

Here the originating sacrifice is performed by gods as well as humans. The world as we know it began with the sacrificial death. Not only the sun, the moon and the wind, but also the hierarchies of mankind, the Indian castes, were part of the original creation.

And Campbell retells the Aztec myth of the goddess Tlalteutli:

"She was alone, the goddess Tlalteutli, walking on the primordial waters—a great and wonderful maiden, with eyes and jaws at every joint that could see and bite like animals. She was observed by the two great gods, Quetzalcoatl, the Plumed Serpent, and Tezcatlipoca, the Smoking Mirror. Deciding to fashion the world of her, they transformed themselves into serpents and came at her from either side. One seized her from the right hand to the left foot, and the other from the left hand to the right foot, and together they ripped her asunder. From the parts they fashioned, not only earth and heavens, but also all the gods. And then to comfort the maiden for what had happened to her, all those gods came down and, paying her obeisance, commanded that there should come from her all the fruits that men require for life. From her hair they made trees, flowers and grass; from her eyes, springs, fountains, and the little caves; from her mouth, rivers and the great caves; from her nose, valleys; and from her shoulders, mountains. But the goddess wept all night, for she had a craving to consume human hearts. And she would not be quiet until they were brought to her. Nor would she bear fruit until she had been drenched with human blood."[8]

Here again, the world as we know it, even the gods themselves, began with a primeval sacrifice. The sacrificial victim is already a sacred being. From her sacrifice come all the beautiful things of the earth: trees, flowers, grass, springs, fountains, caves. And the sacrifice must be repeated, even to the time of Cortez, because the first victim, the goddess, must be "drenched with human blood." So similar are the lessons from ancient creation myths from around the world: from the Native Americans, the Moluccan Islanders, the Indians and the Aztecs.

The Development of the Culture of Sacrifice.

From the culture of sacrifice there developed the primary cultural institutions of the prehistoric world. As long as thirty thousand years ago, humans had developed art, seen in the cave paintings of southern France and Spain, and from these paintings we can infer that humans had already developed myth, ritual and religion.

The selected sacrificial victim must resemble the members of the tribe, so that the catharsis arising from the ritual killing of one of their own could take place. The sacrificial victim must also be different, so that no one would seek revenge for his or her death, and because the victim was already sacred in anticipation of the sacrifice. In many tribes, the chosen sacrificial victim, already a sacred person, was permitted or forced to be king between the time he was chosen and the time of his sacrifice. This sounds very odd, but it was so common and widespread that it took the eminent ethnologist J. G. Frazer twelve volumes to describe its roots and variations in his massive study, *The Golden Bough*.[9]

As the culture of sacrifice matured, some tribes began to accept the practice of substitution for the originally-chosen sacrificial victim. The earliest kings of Egypt were chosen sacred sacrificial victims. At some point a Pharaoh persuaded the priests that he should be permitted to reign, and that another man should be sacrificed in his place. The continuity of leadership which this gave to Egypt greatly increased the powers of Egypt's centralized government.[10] The Pharaoh, still a chosen sacrificial victim, remained a sacred and god-like person to his people, as the Pyramids witness.

In another variation on the theme of substitution, many tribes accepted the substitution of an animal sacrifice for that of a human. Because the sacrificial victim must resemble the members of the tribe in some way, it is probable that the selected animals were caged or penned within the village compound for some period prior to their sacrifice, and encouraged to accept human control and to breed in captivity. The Ainu people of Japan caged and reared bears to be the victims for their sacrificial rituals until recent times. While bears cannot be domesticated, the wild ancestors of cows, pigs, sheep, goats and horses can be. Their capture, confinement and breeding for sacrificial use would and probably did over the course of some centuries lead to the domestication of these animals.[11] It seems more likely than not that the domestication of animals arose as an unforeseen consequence of the requirements of sacrifice. It is hardly likely that primitive tribesmen would decide to capture and raise wild aurochs or boars, the ancestors of cows and pigs, because they knew or hoped that the domesticated descendants of these animals would be useful centuries in the future.

The culture of sacrifice was already ancient when agriculture began and animals were domesticated some eight to ten thousand years ago. These developments permitted the concentration of larger populations in fixed settlements, and the accumulation of wealth, and within a few thousand years the earliest known cities were founded and writing was invented. The most ancient urban civilizations—Sumer, Babylon, and the cities of ancient Egypt, for example—date from that time. All these ancient cities were religious societies, united under a local god or gods. Their religions, expressed in their founding mythologies, were regulated by a priestly class, and included elaborate ritual practices and regulations. They were military societies, led by a king-priest who was also a warrior leader of a warrior class. At the heart of their religions was the sacrifice. These societies were (and of necessity had to be) communities of collective violence, engaged both in continual warfare against neighboring kingdoms and in oppression and subjugation of their own lower classes, women and slaves to the religious and military hierarchy.

The myth-based pagan religions of the culture of sacrifice generally contained no notion that progress was possible. The great Eastern religions, Hinduism, Buddhism, and the more philosophic than religious Confucianism, identified the deity with creation, rather than as a being apart from creation. They supported the hierarchical organization of society, in which each caste or class had specified duties to the others. They generally also took the view that life was not progressive, that the mix of good and evil among men would never change, and that the spiritual goal of the righteous person was either to adapt to this fact and lead an ordered life within the human community, or to detach oneself from life and suffering by ascetic practices leading toward nirvana, or nothing.

The Sacrificial Culture of Israel.

One people, the people of Israel, was different. The civilization and culture of Israel, as described in the Old Testament, is a strange and interesting mixture of the culture of sacrifice and of steps of advance and departure from that culture. All of the culture of sacrifice can be found in Israel. The first human act after the fall of man recorded in Genesis, after the birth of sons to Adam and Eve, is the offering of sacrifice by Cain and Abel. This led to Cain's murder of Abel, following which Cain built a city. The first human community reported in the Bible thus took its foundation from an act of murder arising from a sacrifice.

The God of the early Old Testament is a pagan god, like the gods of the primitive natural religions, angry, tribal, vengeful, and demanding sacrifice. He is constantly changing his mind, like a Greek or Roman god. In Exodus, we read that "The Lord said to Moses, 'I have seen this people, how stiff-necked they are. Now let me alone, so that my wrath may burn hot against them and I may consume them.'" But Moses then made an eloquent speech in defense of his people, reminding God of his earlier promises. "And the Lord changed his mind about the disaster that he planned to bring on his people." Ex. 32, 10, 14. Many Jews and Christians consider it a virtue in Abraham, founder of the Jewish people, that he was willing to commit the worst crime imaginable, the sacrificial murder of his own child, his only son, in service of such a God. Actually, the story of Abraham and Isaac is misunderstood. What it is meant to convey, mythologically, is that the God of Abraham approved the substitution of animal sacrifice for human sacrifice. (The chronology is not correct. Cain and Abel were already offering animal and plant sacrifice long before Abraham. But this is mythology, not chronology.)

Moses founded the people of Israel in internecine slaughter. When the people had offered sacrifice to the golden calf, they "sat down to eat and drink, and rose up to play," and:

> "When Moses saw that the people were running wild (for Aaron had let them run wild, to the derision of their enemies), then Moses stood in the gate of the camp, and said, "Who is on the Lord's side? Come to me!' And all the sons of Levi gathered around him. He said to them, 'Thus says the Lord, the God of Israel, "Put your sword on your side, each of you! Go back and forth from gate to gate throughout the camp, and each of you kill your brother, your friend, and your neighbor."' The sons of Levi did as Moses commanded, and about three thousand of the people fell on that day. Moses said, 'Today you have ordained yourselves for the service of the Lord, each one at the cost of a son or brother, and so have brought a blessing on yourselves this day.'" Ex. 32, 6, 25-29.

The ten commandments, in some versions, are prescriptions of external conduct to be enforced by the sword. "Six days shall work be done, but the seventh day is a sabbath of solemn rest, holy to the Lord; whoever does any work on the sabbath day shall be put to death." Ex. 31, 15.

In the book of Judges, Jephthah, a military leader of Israel, promised God that if God would help him conquer the Ammonites, he would sacrifice to God the first person who came out of the door of his house when he returned victorious. God "gave the Ammonites into his hand." The first person who came out to meet him when he went home was his only child, his daughter (he had doubtless expected to be greeted by a slave). After allowing his daughter two months to wander in the mountains "to bewail her virginity," Jephthah kept his vow, and sacrificed her to God. Judges 11, 29-40. This story of an unwise vow to a trickster God has many counterparts in pagan mythology.

The God of the Old Testament is very different from the Father in heaven described by Jesus. The oldest parts of the Old Testament are very close to the natural religions which arose out of the culture of sacrifice. Ritual sacrifice was always a major element in the culture of the nation of Israel, even to the time of Jesus. The latter part of the book of Exodus, the entire book of Leviticus, and much of the book of Numbers set forth in enormous detail the precise rules and rituals for the priestly sacrifices of the Israelites, and the highly detailed accompanying rules of cleanness and uncleanness. Performance of sacrifice and of the rites of cleanness was reserved to a hereditary priestly caste.

Israel and its tribal God were most united when they were united against the outsider or foreigner. Their God performed the function, like a pagan god, of scourging the enemies of the chosen people. So when the Israelites conquered Palestine the first time, it is written:

"The Lord said to Joshua, Do not fear or be dismayed; take all the fighting men with you, and go up now to Ai. See, I have handed over to you the king of Ai with his people, his city, and his land. You shall do to Ai and his king as you did to Jericho and its king; only its spoil and its livestock you may take as booty for yourselves. Set an ambush against the city, behind it. . . . [there follows the story of the successful ambush] . . . When Israel had finished slaughtering all the inhabitants of Ai in the open wilderness where they pursued them, and when all of them to the very last had fallen by the edge of the sword, all Israel returned to Ai, and attacked it with the edge of the sword. The total of those who fell that day, both men and women, was twelve thousand—all the people of Ai. For Joshua did not draw back his hand, with which he stretched out the sword, until he had utterly destroyed all the inhabitants of Ai. Only the livestock and the spoil of that city Israel took as their booty, according to the word of the Lord that he had issued to Joshua. So Joshua burned Ai, and made it forever a heap of ruins, as it is to this day." Joshua 8, 1-2, 24-28.

This is a pagan tribal god, not the Father in heaven. He was truly called Yahweh Sabaoth—the God of Armies. Israel was deeply rooted in the pagan culture of sacrifice.

And yet there is something different about Israel. Its God is one, not part of his creation, but apart from it. He does not permit images of himself. He made humans in his image, as companions, not slaves. He is a jealous God, permitting no other gods. The true culture of sacrifice does not permit sympathy with the sacrificial victim; yet in the Old Testament the victim is often the hero. Consider Abel, Joseph, Job, the prophets, all of them victims and also innocent heroes. Isaiah speaks against sacrifices:

"What to me is the multitude of your sacrifices? says the Lord; I have had enough of burnt offerings of rams and the fat of fed beasts; I do not delight in the blood of bulls, or of lambs, or of goats. . . . Even though you make many prayers, I will not listen; your hands are full of blood. Wash yourselves; make yourselves clean; remove the evil of your doings before my eyes; cease to do evil, learn to do good; seek justice, rescue the oppressed, defend the orphan, plead for the widow." Isaiah 1, 11, 15-17.

And through the prophet Hosea, the Lord says: "I desire steadfast love and not sacrifice, the knowledge of God rather than burnt offerings." Hos 6, 6. Jesus quoted this verse several times with approval.

Yet even in the books of the prophets the tribal God is intermixed with the universal God. In Isaiah 37, Israel is warring against Assyria:

"Therefore thus says the Lord concerning the king of Assyria: He shall not come into this city, . . . for I will defend this city to save it, for my own sake and for the sake of my servant David. Then the angel of the Lord set out and struck down one hundred eighty-five thousand in the camp of the Assyrians; when morning dawned, they were all dead bodies." Isaiah 37, 33, 35-36.

God's covenant with his chosen people, as developed in the teachings of the prophets, meant that Judaism became a moral religion, with laws which were above and outside political power, and from which political and religious institutions could be criticized. In a way, this was the beginning of the separation of church and state in Western thought. Unlike the religions of India and China, Judaism became a teleological religion, that is, a religion with a direction, a hope of progress, a movement toward a better, more just and more moral society.

The Civilization of Greece and Rome.

The central position of sacrifice, ritual and myth in embodying a nation's culture and history was changed by the emergence of the great classical civilizations of Greece and Rome. In and about the fifth century B.C., the Greeks, principally the Athenians, created many new ways of looking at life, in an incredible flowering of art, philosophy, science and culture which laid the foundations of Western civilization to this day. Their writers invented drama, both tragedy and comedy, and lyric poetry. Their leaders invented democratic politics and political philosophy. Their artists invented classical architecture and sculpture. Their scientists and mathematicians invented arithmetic, geometry, and natural science. Their philosophers invented philosophy, and above and behind all, the value of free and disciplined intellectual inquiry. As the historian J. M. Roberts puts it, "The Greeks invented the philosophical question as part and parcel of one of the great intuitions of all times, that a coherent and logical explanation of things could be found, that the world did not ultimately rest upon the meaningless and arbitrary fiat of gods or demons."[12] And, important for our inquiry, the fifth century Greeks invented history, in the sense not of mythological tales of heroes, or simple annals or chronicles of events, but of rational inquiry and thoughtful narration about actual events in time, in the writings of Herodotus and Thucydides.

But Greek philosophy and history never developed into theology or religion, even as it spread through the Mediterranean world in the Hellenistic and classical Roman cultures. Myth, ritual and sacrifice, which continued in popular culture and practice, was now separated from the progressive intellectual culture of the learned. The attitude of the critical self-reliant man, defiant in the face of the gods (a very modern attitude), had emerged, and mythology and religion would never be the same. That attitude was best and earliest expressed by Aeschylus in his Prometheus trilogy. Prometheus is punished by Zeus for bringing fire to mankind by being chained to a rock for all eternity. Zeus sends a messenger to offer him release if he will repent his crime. Prometheus answers, "I care nothing for Zeus. Let him do what he will."[13] The foundations of modern culture were laid down in Athens in the fifth century B.C., and the natural religions of myth and ritual were permanently weakened.

The Roman empire, united under Caesar Augustus (31 B.C.-

14 A.D.), ruled over the entire Mediterranean world. While the Greek genius was intellectual, the Roman genius was in administration, military power, engineering, law and governance. Under Roman rule, communication and travel within the empire became commonplace, and a cosmopolitan Mediterranean culture grew. There was within the empire an enormous variety of religious and ritual practices, from festivals of agricultural deities to philosophical monotheism to the cult of the emperor, most of them generally tolerated; the Roman empire has been described as a world full of gods.[14] Roman religion "had nothing to do with individual salvation and not much with individual behavior."[15]

The Problem of the Culture of Sacrifice.

We have seen how the culture of sacrifice developed and rooted itself in human civilization from the most primitive times to the highly developed ancient civilizations of the time of Jesus. We are now in a position to see generally both how the culture of sacrifice made its essential contribution to the growth of human culture, and how the culture of sacrifice has limited humanity's further growth.

The culture of sacrifice was humanity's first great invention. It was the indispensable invention, because it provided the mechanisms necessary to bring the evolved genetic behaviors of the earliest humans under social control. Without these mechanisms of control, the earliest humans could not have organized themselves in groups large enough to develop and preserve the later ancient inventions of human civilization; they would have killed each other first. From the primeval sacrifice came the first prohibitions and taboos, the first rituals and myths. Larger communities could be organized and united with the binding agent of the sacrificial religion. Community-enforced taboos kept violence in check within each community and directed it outward. Such communities could protect and feed themselves. So universal and ancient is the culture of sacrifice that it seems that tribes which did not invent it (or adopt it from tribes which did) simply did not survive.

Under the social control of sacrificial religions, humanity was able slowly to spread throughout the world and to develop the other fundamental inventions of human civilization: tools, agriculture, domestication of animals, organized military forces, writing, money, art and literature. The life of communities became more complex, division of labor was discovered, and the first great cities and nations emerged. As social and governmental institutions were developed and elaborated, societies gradually became less wholly dependent on the prohibitions and rules of their sacrificial religions to maintain social order. Upon reaching a certain level of development, ancient nations would develop some form of a criminal justice system; the critical point was reached when the governing authority had developed the power not only to apprehend and punish the offender, but also to prevent the injured party or his kin from taking private revenge. An organized military force would take over the external projections of the nation's violence. A legal system would develop to protect the rights of property-owners to their wealth, their wives and their slaves, and to arbitrate disputes. The sacrificial religion and its priests gradually reduced their activities to a less central but still necessary function. As even the most despotic of governments depends for its power on the support of key members of the nation, and the acquiescence or acceptance of the rest, the maintenance of the nation's mythology and rituals remained important. The religion of sacrifice still provided the mythology or ideology which allowed the people to feel that they were one united people, different from and superior to the barbarians or enemies which surrounded them.

In the Mediterranean world, Israel had remained a small theocracy. In Greece, the religions of sacrifice were still practiced, but they were separated from the higher culture and intellectual life of the nation. And in Rome at the time of Caesar Augustus there were a great many cults and sects of religion and sacrifice, and the unity of the empire was based not on a common religion but on Roman military power, wealth, and effective civil administration. The culture of sacrifice had run its course; it had completed its great contribution to the progress of humanity.

But the lives of most men and women living within the culture of sacrifice, or in the ancient nations built on the foundation of sacrificial religions, were far from satisfactory. The internal discipline and cohesion of these nations were bought at a price. There was little room left for individual initiative or self-direction, except among the very wealthy. Suppression of internal dissension and violence was heavy and brutal. Suspicion, fear, envy and greed toward outsiders or enemies led to frequent violent warfare between communities or nations. The hierarchical stratification of societies had hardened into caste systems, with the suppression of women and with slaves at the bottom. The virtues of humanity's childhood and adolescence had become the vices of humanity's maturity. The virtues of the most successful primitive tribes had been the controlled direction of violence away from other members of the tribe and onto outsiders, enforced ritual prohibitions and practices, and a rigorously hierarchical social system, all founded in a vigorous sacrificial religion. These virtues had served their limited purposes. Their time had passed. They had become vices, locking societies into the suppression of individual independence and initiative, regular persecution of the downtrodden or those seen as "different" or "other," and endless war against other tribal, ethnic, cultural or religious communities.

The ultimate problem of humanity was this: the evolutionary stability of the culture of sacrifice and the cultures of the nations founded on its principles had become the principal obstacle to the continued development of humanity. The culture of sacrifice itself had accepted and retained as its primary constituents the anti-social animal behaviors built into the genetic material of all humans by natural selection. The culture of sacrifice had incorporated violence into its central ritual of sacrifice; it had incorporated racial, ethnic and national hatred into its mythologies; it had incorporated acquisitiveness and dominant-submissive behavior into its hierarchical structures. There was no basis within the culture of sacrifice to modify or eradicate these behaviors without destroying the culture of sacrifice itself. And these fundamental behaviors, with the combined forces of biological evolution and cultural evolution behind them, have remained extraordinarily resistant to change.

At this time, in the reign of Caesar Augustus, Jesus of Nazareth was born. To the Christian, this is the crucial intervention of God in the affairs of humanity. Our goal is to discover why he came, and what his mission was. My thesis is that he came to make possible the continued development of humanity toward its destiny or goal. His principal contribution would be to show how the otherwise immovable obstacle presented by the culture of sacrifice can and must be overcome.

Notes:
1. Freud, Sigmund, *Totem and Taboo* (Vintage Books, 1946), p. 172 (Emphasis added).
2. Girard, René, *Violence and the Sacred* (Johns Hopkins University Press, 1977); *Things Hidden Since the Foundation of the World* (Stanford University Press, 1987); *The Scapegoat* (Johns Hopkins University Press, 1986). I am deeply indebted to Girard for his theory of the culture of sacrifice.
3. Girard, René, *Violence and the Sacred, supra,* p. 27.
4. Axelrod, Robert, *The Evolution of Cooperation* (Basic Books, 1984), p. 93.
5. Campbell, Joseph, *Historical Atlas of World Mythology* (Harper & Row, 1988), Vol. II, Part 2, p. 177.
6. Campbell, Joseph, *The Masks of God: Primitive Mythology* (Viking Press, 1970), pp. 173 ff.
7. Embree, Ainslee T., ed., *The Hindu Tradition* (Vintage Books, 1972), pp. 25-26.
8. Campbell, Joseph, *Historical Atlas of World Mythology* (Harper & Row, 1988), Vol. II, Part 1, p. 37.
9. Frazer, James George, *The Golden Bough*, one volume abridged (MacMillan Company, 1963).

10. Campbell, Joseph, *The Masks of God: Oriental Mythology* (Viking Press, 1970), pp. 73-74.
11. Girard, René, *Violence and the Sacred, supra,* pp. 68-73.
12. Roberts, J. M., *The Penguin History of the World* (Penguin Books, 1995), p. 192.
13. Aeschylus, *Prometheus Bound,* Vol. 8, The Harvard Classics (P.F. Collier & Son, 1909), p. 200.
14. Hopkins, Keith, *A World Full of Gods* (Penguin Putnam, 2001).
15. Roberts, J. M., *The Penguin History of the World, supra,* p. 245.

IV

The Person of Jesus.

The Sources.

Jesus lived in historical times. For almost five hundred years, the practice of recording human words and deeds in histories rather than in myths had been established and had spread throughout the Mediterranean world. The replacement of mythology with history was a major advance. There is an enormous difference in accuracy as well as in reliable detail between what we know of the Trojan war and what we know of the Peloponnesian war, between what we know of Romulus and Remus and what we know of Julius Caesar and Caesar Augustus. This is important, because it means that when the Gospels were written, the writers knew what history was, and how to do it. On any kind of examination, the Gospels appear to be written as historical narratives, not devotional, mystical or theological accounts. While they do not follow modern biographical formats or conform to modern standards of history, nothing else from the civilizations of Greece or Rome does either.

The life of Jesus and the life of the early Christian communities are well-documented, compared to our sources for most of ancient history. We have no fewer than four separate narratives, or Gospels, of Jesus's public life and death, a history of the early Christian Church in the Acts of the Apostles, and twenty-one letters by the early followers of Jesus in the canonical New Testament alone. The Gospels, the Acts and the Epistles were all written between about 45 A.D. and 105 A. D., or between fifteen and seventy-five years after Jesus's death, by individuals directly or indirectly connected to him.[1] This is a substantial amount of contemporary documentation for ancient times. As a comparison, for the Roman emperor Tiberius, who lived at roughly the same time, we have biographies by Velleius Paterculus, Tacitus, Suetonius and Dio Cassius, only the first of whom was directly connected to him; the others wrote from seventy-five to two hundred years after his death.[2]

For the last two centuries, the Gospels have been subjected to severe historical and literary criticism. Now I do not believe that scripture in general, or the Gospels in particular, were inspired by God or written at the dictation of the Holy Spirit. To me, they are ordinary historical documents, and as such must be subject to ordinary historical criticism and analysis. But I also do not believe that they should be criticized more skeptically than other historical documents of their time. Among the criticisms raised by some scripture scholars are the following:

1.   The Gospels are not modern biographies. Setting aside the infancy narratives in Matthew and Luke, they all begin the story of Jesus with the beginning of his public teaching life, and say nothing about his adolescence and young adult life prior to that time. It is not clear from the Gospels how long Jesus's period of public teaching was. John records that during his public life Jesus went to Jerusalem three different times for the Passover; the other Gospels record only one journey to Jerusalem. The teachings of Jesus are not set forth in the Gospels in the order in which they were given, but are more or less grouped by subject matter or style. Matthew groups many ethical teachings in the Sermon on the Mount, Chapters 5 through 7; apocalyptic teachings in Chapter 24; denunciations of the Pharisees in Chapter 23; and so forth. I do not see that any of this presents a problem about the credibility of what is reported in the Gospels. There is

a fair amount of information which we don't have, but that doesn't affect the accuracy of what we do have.

2.   Some scholars have made much of minor inconsistencies. In the story of Peter's denial of Jesus, did the cock crow once (Mt 26, 74-75), or twice (Mk 14, 72)? Did Matthew or Luke set forth the "original" version of the Lord's Prayer? This also does not seem to me to raise a problem of credibility. Anyone who has listened closely to the testimony of witnesses at a trial knows that minor inconsistencies always occur, even between eyewitnesses. It would be the absence of minor inconsistencies, not their presence, which would raise suspicion.

3.   Some scholars are concerned with the period between the time the events took place and the time, thirty to seventy years later, when the present Gospels were finally composed and assembled. How could the exact words of Jesus have been preserved orally for such a length of time? I think there are several reasons why we should not be concerned with this time delay:

(a) In ancient and medieval times before the invention of printing, skills of memorization were taught and practiced to a level of achievement we can only imagine. This was particularly true in Israel at the time of Jesus. It is true in some orthodox Jewish schools and in many Islamic schools to this day. Memorizing a narrative the length of a Gospel would not be an unusual feat for a scholar at any orthodox Jewish or Islamic school.

(b) Jesus taught and preached on a daily basis throughout Judea and Galilee for several years. Although his teaching varied, he undoubtedly repeated himself regularly; he must have had a "stump speech." The disciples followed him from place to place. They certainly heard the same teachings, the same stump speech, over and over. Memorizing the stump speech would be easy. (This would also explain in part some of the minor variances in wording of the same text in different Gospels; different writers had simply memorized different hearings of the same speech.) The fact that much of the teaching was presented in memorable stories and with memorable illustrations would have made accurate memorization much easier. The disciples were men and women who had left all to follow Jesus. One may assume they were paying close attention.

4. Some scholars assert that much of the writing of the Gospels was composed in response to the needs of the early Christian communities in which the Gospel writer lived. I think this is a way of explaining and concealing the *a priori* disbelief of the scholar: he is able to say, for example, that the community needed miracle stories to evidence and bear witness to their faith in Jesus, and thus discount the testimonial evidence that the miracles had actually occurred. This allows the scholar to disbelieve in miracles and yet avoid the professional embarrassment of having to throw out more than half of Mark's Gospel, the oldest of the four Gospels. I will address the question whether Jesus could and did work miracles near the end of this chapter.

In my own reflections on questions about whether the Gospels are substantially accurate historical records of the public life, the teachings, the death and the resurrection of Jesus, the following considerations seemed to me to have great weight:

1. The Gospels were regarded from the time of their composition as accurate historical records, and are entitled to the respect for the text which historians and scholars give to ancient documents and records generally.

2. Jesus, as described in the Gospels, is such an extraordinarily innovative and creative person that, if he had not lived substantially as he is portrayed, no one could have made him up. As he is described in the Gospels, Jesus was commanding in his personal presence. Men whom he called to follow him left their jobs and their wives and followed him. He spoke with great assurance and command. There was no hesitation or doubt in his teaching. He was subtle, clever and powerful in controversy.

3. The teachings of Jesus were unique. Jesus set out a new morality, contrasting it with traditional morality, and he set the highest moral standards known to our civilization. He rejected the old rules, and established new ideals. He challenged the authority of the rulers of his people (religious rulers, because Israel

was then a theocracy). His unwavering opposition to their religious rule eventually brought them to have him ignominiously executed, but his teaching and example survived, triumphed, and spread throughout the world. The force of his personality, living on in the memory of those who had known him, inspired an extraordinary growth in the early Christian communities, which spread throughout the Mediterranean world within a very few generations after his death. It seems to me to be ridiculous to think that this kind of originality in teaching and example could have been invented by a group of disciples or by the early Christian communities.

4. An important quality of the teaching of Jesus is the extraordinary rhetorical and literary power of expression which he commanded. In my view, this is not insignificant, and it is not a merely aesthetic judgment. When one reads Shakespeare, one is struck by the enormous literary power of the man, to speak so profoundly of the human condition and to reach so deeply into the human heart. Because of this ability, we regard Shakespeare as one of the greatest, if not the greatest, of the writers of our civilization, and as a genius from whom we learn much about life.

So it is with the teachings of Jesus. His knowledge of the human heart and soul, and his command of rhetorical and literary means of expression which he used to reach the hearts and souls of his followers, was extraordinary and unique. His command of metaphor, and of the extended metaphor of parable, shows that he was greatly gifted in his ability to set forth his teachings in ways men and women could grasp, remember, and apply to their lives, whatever their level of education and experience. The suggestion that this body of teaching could have been composed one or two generations after his death by various writers in response to the needs of their various local Christian communities is ludicrous. One can no more believe that than believe that a committee of Jacobean writers sat down in 1620 and composed the eighteen Shakespeare plays which appeared in print for the first time in the First Folio in 1623. Works of literary genius cannot be composed by committee.

Indeed, a reading of some of the apocryphal Christian writings of the first or early second centuries shows that many of the sayings of Jesus attributed to him, but not contained in the four canonical Gospels (and therefore arguably written by other writers, or a committee), have none of the cogency and the force of Jesus's authentic teachings. For example, in the Gospel of Thomas, Saying 11 reads as follows:

> "Jesus said, 'This heaven will pass away, and the one above it will pass away. The dead are not alive, and the living will not die. During the days when you ate what is dead, you made it come alive. When you are in the light, what will you do? On the day when you were one, you became two. But when you become two, what will you do?'"

What on earth can that mean? Or take Saying 59, which reads:

> "Jesus said: Look to the living one as long as you live, otherwise you must die and then try to see the living one, and you will be unable to see."[3]

The differences between the authentic teachings of Jesus and the sayings of those trying to imitate him are apparent to anyone with an ear for style or a sense for substance. Thomas Cahill describes the singular stylistic unity of the Gospels this way:

> "In nothing is their unity so evident as in their portrayal of Jesus. Though he is presented in various lights and shadows, depending on the concerns, personality, and skill of each author, he exudes even under this treatment a remarkable consistency, so that we feel on finishing his story, whether it is told well or badly, simply or extravagantly, that we know the man—and that in each telling he is identifiably the same man. This phenomenon

of consistency beneath the differences makes Jesus a unique figure in world literature: never have so many writers managed to convey the same impression of the same human being over and over again. More than this, Jesus—what he says, what he does—is almost always comprehensible to the reader, who needs no introduction, no scholarly background, to penetrate the meaning of Jesus's words and actions. The Sermon on the Mount, the Good Samaritan, the Washing of the Feet, the Empty Tomb: all these and many more gestures, instructions, and symbols are immediately intelligible not only to the simplest reader but even to the unlettered and the immature.

"There is no other body of literature approaching its two thousandth birthday of which the same may be said."[4]

So I have concluded that the Gospels are substantially accurate recountings of the words and deeds of Jesus. This conclusion seems to me to be grounded in the evidence and in my experience, and to be sound and reasonable. Just to be on the safe side, however, I feel more confident about the teachings which are repeated over and over by Jesus, so that the possibility of inauthenticity is even more remote.

Jesus the Person—the Theological Tradition.

What kind of a person was Jesus? The traditional Christian teaching is that Jesus is both God and man. I have tried to understand how this could be. In thinking about this question, one can either start with the idea that Jesus is God, and try to understand how he is also a man, or start with the idea that he is a man, and try to understand in what way he is also God. (A caution to the reader: Take the next four pages slowly. It is classical Christian theology, but it is highly and densely philosophical, and it may be difficult for those who are not trained in this kind of analytical thinking. If you get bogged down, fast-forward to the next section.)

Traditional Christian teaching begins with the idea that Jesus is God. This is the case with Anselm's explanation, as we have seen. The traditional explanation of the person of Jesus begins with the doctrine of the Holy Trinity: there is God the Father, God the Son, and God the Holy Spirit, from all eternity. Humanity has separated itself from God the Father by Adam's sin. God the Son then decides to redeem humanity by taking on human form and offering his life as a perfect sacrifice to God the Father. But here is where the problem begins. If we think of Jesus by starting with the idea of Jesus as God, or as a Person of God, it becomes very difficult for us to have any understanding of or identification with his real human life.

Take, for example, the act of knowing something. The central experience of human life is having a definite limited individual and personal consciousness, extended over time, so that at one moment one object of thought or perception is included in consciousness, and at another moment one is conscious of another object. But the divine consciousness is omniscient. God simultaneously knows everything that can be known about all things. He knows every path of every electron in every one of the 10^{79} atoms in the universe, from the origin of the universe to its end, and he knows this all at once. If subatomic particles vibrate like strings, he knows every vibration of every string. His knowledge is wholly unlike human knowledge. God does not observe events or analyze data; he does not reflect on what he has learned, nor does he learn. He knows all that is, directly and immediately, because his knowledge is as universal as his power. He fully understands, all at the same time, all the relationships between all beings and all the implications of their powers and limitations, and he knows all these things at once. How could Jesus experience that way of knowing things, that kind of consciousness, and still be a human person with a human life?

The classic theological answer is that Jesus was one person with two natures, one divine and one human. But this answer seems to raise more problems than it solves. The critical distinction between "person" and "nature" is a slippery distinction which seems to dissolve under examination. I cannot grasp the concept of a "person," an individual self-identity or constant unity of conscious life, which is neither human nor divine, but which can become either (or both) depending on whether it unites with a human set of powers, attributes and qualities or a divine set of powers, attributes and qualities. The more one thinks about it, the more elusive the explanation becomes, until it dissolves into a formula of words which contains no meaning.

The concept of "human nature," as used in this classical Christian theology, is an obsolete and disproven way of thinking about the human species. It is what Ernst Mayr calls typological thinking, or essentialism. As Mayr describes it,

> "Essentialism was the almost universally held worldview from the ancients until Darwin's time. Founded by the Pythagoreans and Plato, essentialism taught that all seemingly variable phenomena of nature could be sorted into classes. Each class is characterized by its definition (its essence). This essence is constant (invariable) and sharply demarcated against all other such essences. . . . A species was considered by the essentialist to be such a class and was referred to by the philosophers as a natural kind . . . . Darwin showed that one simply could not understand evolution as long as one accepted essentialism. Species and populations are not types, they are not essentialistically defined classes, but rather are biopopulations composed of genetically unique individuals."[5]

"Human nature" is then not an essence; it is simply an informal description or reference to the group of characteristics which members of the human species, or the human biopopulation, have in common. I do not "have" a human nature; I am a genetically unique human being. "Human nature" simply describes the fact that I am very much like you or like any other person. My "personhood" is human. I have no personhood, no continuing conscious self-identity, apart from being a human being. So if Jesus was truly man, he was a human person. He was not a floating person, neither human nor divine, but capable of becoming either by uniting with a human or divine nature, because there is no such thing.

If Jesus was both divine and human, did he have both a divine will and a human will? If he had one will, was it divine, in which case his humanity was incomplete, or was it human, in which case the divine nature was incomplete? If Jesus had two wills, would there not be two persons, two independent continuing conscious self-identities, even if the two wills always agreed? What Jesus said about this was, "I have come from heaven, not to do my own will, but to do the will of the one who sent me." Jn 6, 38. If this means anything, it means Jesus had a human will, and God the Father had a different will, which Jesus did not call "my own." Similarly, if Jesus had two intellects, one a human intellect, which sees things one at a time and proceeds from one thing to another, and the other a divine intellect, which sees and understands all things all at once and does not change, how could these have coexisted in the same person without the divine intellect wholly blotting out the human?

What actually happens is that, in the mind of the Christian believer, the formula of "one person with two natures" is accepted and not examined, and Jesus is simply thought of as God the Son, the Second Person of the Holy Trinity. Since the Second Person of the Holy Trinity is God from all eternity, it is this divine Person, God the Son, who after being in heaven for a long time takes on human form in the person of Jesus, and Jesus can no longer be understood as a real man.

I find this description of the Incarnation of Jesus hard to distinguish from the stories in Ovid's *Metamorphoses*, where gods often took human or animal form when they came down from Olympus to deal with ordinary humans, or from the science fiction stories, like the *X-Files*, in which an alien takes on the appearance of a human being. Donald Bloesch, following this line of thinking, has described the nature of Jesus as follows:

> "Jesus is humanly personal *but has no independent human existence*, since the center of his being is the Word of God, the second Person of the Trinity. . . . Jesus Christ must not be thought of as being autonomous or self-existent. God is the acting subject, and the manhood of Jesus is the predicate of the Godhead. This means that Jesus Christ differs from other men in kind and not simply in degree. He is set apart from the human race in that his origin is in heaven. . . . He lived among us and died as one of us, and yet *he was qualitatively different from us*."[6]

This is Jesus as the automaton of God. This view simply puts an unbridgeable gulf between Jesus and the rest of us humans.

It is traditional Christian doctrine that Jesus is a true man as well as true God. I think that if we lose sight of his genuine humanity, we will not see him as an example, or understand his mission, or feel the attraction of the call to imitate him. If we do not believe that Jesus is a real human person, like us, we will not really believe that his example can be followed by real human people like us. It is not enough to simply assert, as the Nicene Creed does, that the Son of God, begotten of the Father before all ages, became man and was truly man. This leads to the confusions and contradictions described above. Some Christian theologians have tried to deal with this problem by teaching that the divine attributes of Jesus were hidden, or became "quiescent," during Jesus's life. But this simply leads us back to the notion of a god in metamorphosis, a god in disguise, a deceptive god. We need a point of departure different from that of classical Christian theology to understand Jesus. A good place to start, it seems to me, is with Jesus's own words about himself and his relationship with God.

What Jesus Said About Himself.

The Gospel of St. John contains many more sayings of Jesus about himself and his personal relationship with God the Father than do the other Gospels. Here are a few of these astonishing sayings; consider them slowly and thoughtfully:

> "I came from God and now I am here. I did not come on my own, but he sent me." Jn 8, 42.

> "If you loved me, you would rejoice that I am going to the Father, because the Father is greater than I." Jn 14, 28.

> "The works that my Father has given me to complete, the very works that I am doing, testify on my behalf that the Father has sent me." Jn 5, 36.

> "I can do nothing on my own. As I hear, I judge; and my judgment is just, because I seek to do not my own will, but the will of him who sent me." Jn 5, 30.

> "I judge no one. Yet even if I do judge, my judgment is valid; for it is not I alone who judge, but I and the Father who sent me. In your law it is written that the testimony of two witnesses is valid. I testify on my own behalf, and the Father who sent me testifies on my behalf." Jn 8, 15-18.

> "The Son can do nothing on his own, but only what he sees the Father doing; for whatever the Father does, the Son does likewise. The Father loves the Son and shows him all that he himself is doing; and he will show him greater works than these, so that you will be astonished." Jn 5, 19-20.

> "My food is to do the will of him who sent me and to complete his work." Jn 4, 34.

"Everything that the Father gives me will come to me, and anyone who comes to me I will never drive away; for I have come down from heaven, not to do my own will, but the will of him who sent me. And this is the will of him who sent me, that I should lose nothing of all that he has given me, but raise it up on the last day. This is indeed the will of my Father, that all who see the Son and believe in him may have eternal life; and I will raise them up on the last day." Jn 6, 37-40.

"Everyone who has heard and learned from the Father comes to me. No one has seen the Father except the one who is from God; he has seen the Father." Jn 6, 45-46.

"The Father and I are one." Jn 10, 30.

"The Father is in me and I am in the Father." Jn 10, 38.

"I am the way, and the truth, and the life. No one comes to the Father except through me. If you know me, you will know my Father also. From now on, you do know him and have seen him." Jn 14, 6-7.

For the most part, as we see, Jesus describes himself as a human person, sent by God, whom he always calls the Father. The Father is greater than Jesus. Jesus can do nothing on his own. The Father is a different person. The testimony of Jesus and the separate testimony of the Father, manifest in Jesus's miracles, is the testimony of two different witnesses. Jesus has his own will, a human will, and the Father has a different will, the divine will. "I seek to do not my own will, but the will of him who sent me." Jesus has a direct perception of the Father and what the Father is doing, but in a way which the human mind can receive, in parts and as needed, not in one overwhelming blast of omniscience. "The Father loves the Son and shows him all that he himself is doing; *and he will show him greater works than these . . . .*" Jesus does not know everything that God knows. When talking about the last days of the world, Jesus himself said, "But about that day and hour no one knows, neither the angels of heaven, *nor the Son*, but only the Father." Mt 24, 36.

But Jesus also describes his relationship with the Father as unique among all humans for all time. "No one has seen the Father except the one who is from God; *he has seen the Father*." Jesus alone provides the path, and is the path, by which men may reach God. "I am the way, and the truth, and the life. No one comes to the Father except through me." And Jesus describes this unique relationship between him and his Father as a real union. "The Father is in me and I am in the Father." "The Father and I are one."

There is a balance which we must maintain in talking and thinking about Jesus. We need to understand that he was really a human person with a fully human life, and that this human life was not overwhelmed by divine power. But we also need to understand that he was not just one of the many holy persons who have received, or who have believed they have received, a special revelation from God, and have set about teaching and doing good works based on that revelation. Jesus's own sayings show how difficult the balance is; sometimes he speaks of himself as human—"I can do nothing on my own"; and sometimes he speaks of himself as God—"Before Abraham came to be, I am." We need to wrestle with the identity of Jesus in order to understand his mission, and we need to start somewhere, either with the idea of Jesus as God, the Second Person of the Holy Trinity, or Jesus as a human person.

I propose to start with the idea of Jesus as a human person, and work toward his relationship with God, for two reasons. First, in his unique combination of human and divine powers, it is the humanity of Jesus which is fragile and gets lost, and I believe that having a firm grasp on that humanity is essential to understanding his mission and our response to his mission. Second, we must begin with the Gospels, and there we find a man; a good man, a holy man, even an awe-inspiring man; but also a man who grew up in a village, traveled around with his followers doing his work, went to weddings and dinner parties, and was at different times angry, happy, calm, and mournful at the death of a friend.

The God-Consciousness of Jesus.

The explanation of Jesus's person and life developed by Friedrich Schleiermacher (1768-1834), a nineteenth century German theologian, is the most satisfactory explanation I have found.[7] It is not perfect, but I believe it coheres more closely to Jesus's own description of his relation to his Father than any other, and it enables us to make better sense of Jesus's life than we can with any other explanation of that relationship.

Schleiermacher begins with the idea that many people have an interior awareness of one's own absolute and complete dependence on an "other," who is himself absolute and not dependent on anything outside himself. He calls this the faculty of God-consciousness. At times, this awareness is felt as a sense of piety or reverence; at times, it is felt as the source of one's conscience, one's consciousness of moral and ethical demands placed on us by an absolute and perfect "other." This awareness is dim in all of us; it comes and it goes. Most of us are only conscious of it during the few moments of quiet reflection and contemplation we find in our busy schedules, and some of us are not conscious of it at all. But I believe it is there, a consciousness of God, in all of us, at least as something which can be discovered and developed. It is not, however, strong enough in any of us to keep us free from sin, error, or bad judgment.

In Jesus, alone of all humans, this faculty of God-consciousness was full; it was at the maximum level which is compatible with and does not destroy real human life; and it was at that level throughout his life. This is the miracle of the Incarnation: Jesus, an ordinary human being, was chosen by God and given at birth a consciousness of God similar to, but at a different level of magnitude than, that of any other human. It is as if, for all the rest of us, consciousness is a darkened room which gradually fills with light as we mature, and there is a little aperture, like a camera shutter, in one wall which opens from time to time, and through which we have a consciousness of God and his presence, but intermittently, and always as through a glass, darkly. In Jesus, the shutter is wide, clear, and always open, and he always sees God. This capacity is an expansion of a truly human capacity, so it does not make Jesus less fully human, although in Jesus, unlike us, the power of his God-consciousness was sufficiently strong that it made him permanently free from sin, from error, and from bad judgment. Jesus recognized this power from the outset as unique to him, and this is the power he described when he said of himself, "No one has seen the Father except the one who is from God; *he has seen the Father.*"

The God-consciousness of Jesus did not override his human intelligence and his growth as a human personality. St. Luke's Gospel records that "Jesus increased in wisdom and in years, and in divine and human favor." Lk 2, 52. Tales of miracles performed by the infant Jesus are told in the apocryphal gospels, but nowhere in the accepted canonical scriptures. Jesus did not know all that God knows, in the way which God knows it, because that activity cannot be performed by a human intelligence, but he saw all things, with his human intelligence and vision, from the earliest moments of life, in the light of his God-consciousness, in the light of the presence of God within him. In biological terms (not drawn from Schleiermacher), Jesus's cerebral cortex, with the guidance of his God-consciousness, was always in control of his limbic system, without effort or struggle. This implies that he could not sin, and that in a real sense he could not be tempted to sin. That is to say, a real temptation implies a real possibility that the tempted person will give in to the temptation. Jesus's God-consciousness was so full and so open at all times that the possibility that he could ignore his God-consciousness and commit sin was never real. Jesus proceeded from innocence to virtue and merit, without sin. As he learned about sin and error by living a normal life and observing and interacting with other people, he became conscious of the fact that he was unique among human beings in his fully-developed God-consciousness and the powers that accompanied it.

Another way of imagining what this must have been like is to think of Jesus as always hearing the voice of God in his head, teaching him, counseling him, warning him, consoling him. As each of us carries on a sort of interior dialogue with oneself, more or less continuing throughout our waking hours, so Jesus was able to carry on an interior dialogue with God at all times, and God was really there participating in the dialogue. As Jesus thought like a human, in a discursive, progressive, rational way, which is not how God knows things, so, in a way, Jesus was engaged throughout his life in the continuous translation of God's thought and will into human thought and human language.

The contemporary English Catholic theologian James Alison expresses this understanding of Jesus in only slightly different language:

> "Jesus was able to answer the Sadducees in the way he did because *his* imagination and heart were not darkened, senseless, futile [like those of the rest of humanity]. That is to say, he did not share the condition of the human heart in which, according to St. Paul, we all share. This was not because he was not human, nor because he was God instead of being human, but because his fully human imagination was capable of being fixed on the ineffable effervescence and vivacity, power and deathlessness of God in a way which seems almost unimaginable to us."[8]

Jesus's intellectual development took place in the normal human way, but because he had the light of God's presence within him, he saw things more clearly and more deeply, and without error. In the only story of Jesus's youth found in the Gospels, he went with his parents to the Passover festival in Jerusalem when he was twelve. After the festival was over, he stayed behind, and after three days he was found with the teachers in the temple, "listening to them and asking them questions; and all those who heard him were astounded at his intelligence and his replies." When his mother scolded him for staying behind, he answered, "Why were you looking for me? Did you not know that I must be about my Father's business?" Lk 2, 46-49. We see here an exceptionally bright young student of the law and of the Jewish religion, but not a deity in disguise; a twelve-year-old who could get a scolding from his mother; but already someone who called God his Father, which was part of his new and revolutionary way of teaching about God. We also see developing in him at an early age his consciousness of his mission. It was his duty to do everything only in the light of his God-consciousness, and in the light of the divine will present in a unique way within him. As he was faithful and constant in this duty, God acted and operated through him. "I can do nothing on my own. As I hear, I judge; and my judgment is just, because I seek to do not my own will, but the will of him who sent me." Jn 5, 30.

Jesus next appears (and, for Mark and John, first appears) at the beginning of his public ministry, having waited, in accordance with custom, until his thirtieth year. What we read of his activity during his public ministry is consistent with what we would expect of a person with his singular God-consciousness and his unique vision, with the vision of God and the will of God within him, and with his clear perception of the lack of this consciousness, vision and will in the rest of the world. He would use his efforts to communicate to others his unique vision of life in the light of the will of God, which he called the Kingdom of Heaven, in contrast to the life of the world. He desired nothing other than the transformation of the world from the world of the culture of sacrifice into the Kingdom of Heaven, and he desired to do it by means of pure self-communication. He would communicate himself, his personal vision, his unique ethical imperatives and his consciousness of God, by word and by personal example. He would set forth for others what they must do to separate from the "world," overcome the world's culture of sacrifice, and enter the Kingdom of Heaven. He taught that what men and women must do to enter the Kingdom of Heaven is to accept his communication of self, to believe and trust in him and his word, and to identify with him and follow his teaching and example. Ultimately, Jesus's teaching is not rules, or propositions of faith, or rituals; it is his personal life. This is what he meant when he said, "I *am* the way, and the truth, and the life. No one comes to the Father except through me. If you know me, you will know my Father also. From now on, you do know him and have seen him." Jn 14, 6-7.

In the sense I have just described, Jesus is true God and true man. His human mind, his human will and his human consciousness were filled with the consciousness of God, but they were not overwhelmed by it. He could and did distinguish between his own will and "the will of him who sent me." But Jesus was fully united at all times with God his Father. "The Father is in me and I am in the Father." "The Father and I are one." Jesus is truly God.

Did Jesus Live Before His Conception?

Was Jesus truly God before Jesus was born? This is a trick question, like the question whether God can make a weight so heavy he cannot lift it. The question can only be answered if we first correctly understand what it means to say that God is eternal.

God is all-perfect, and without any limits on his existence and powers. As God is not limited by space, so he is not limited by time. It is hard to think of time as a limitation, because we have no experience of anything which does not experience the passage of time. Let's take this slowly; it turns out to be very important. When I reflect on my own life, I am conscious that my life and my being is never completely possessed by me all at once, but in parts which precede and follow one another. This is true of all of us and of all we know. Time is change, or the measure of change. I am not now the person I once was, nor am I the person I will be tomorrow. Time is a fundamental limitation upon one's possession of one's existence. Time does not limit God. Woody Allen once said that "Time is nature's way of keeping everything from happening at once." With God, everything does happen at once. God himself is perfect and does not change. As time is only the measure of change, time has no meaning with God. This is not altered by God's creation of a universe which changes and which does exist in time. God remains outside of time.

This concept is so counter-intuitive that we need to consider it more closely or we will instinctively and erroneously place God back into time. Imagination can be misleading, but I find some help in imagining the time line of the universe projected onto a very large semicircular movie screen, with God as the audience (and producer and director too) watching the whole show at once. God can see all that was and all that is and all that will be at the same time, because it's all on the screen (his screen) at the same time. God is completely present at any point in time in the life of the universe, but he is not thereby limited to that point in time. Since he can see the whole screen at once, he is fully present at all points in its time, without being a part of time. It follows that God does not have a memory, nor does he have prescience, or knowledge of the future as future. God does not foresee what is to happen. God only has "now," and everything is "now" to God.

The instinctive human tendency to place God in time creates problems in thinking about God which do not exist if we hold firmly to the concept of God's being outside of time. For example, the Nicene Creed speaks of the Son as "born of the Father *before* all ages" ("*ante omnia saecula*") and the beginning of the Gospel of St. John is that "In the beginning *was* the Word." Both of these verbal formulas imply that God the Son spent some time as God alone before he took on human form in Jesus. Actually, he didn't. God does not spend time. He is always in the present, and he does not change. From God's point of view, Jesus is always born, always lives, always dies, and always rises again. It is all in the present for God. God is always now united with Jesus, who is born and who now lives, and there is not a time for God when the Son of God was not also a real living human person. This means that if Jesus is the Word, of whom John spoke, and of whom he said, "All things came into being through him, and without him not one thing came into being," Jesus the man, who, from God's perspective, is always born and always lives, was there when all things came into being. It is not consistent with the concept of God's eternity to believe that there were divine activities the Son of God engaged in before the birth of Jesus. We should therefore not think of God the Son as living for a long time before Jesus's birth, and then putting on the form of a human being for a time, and then going back to being God, so that Jesus is thought of more as a God in disguise than as a real man. The Son of God is always and eternally Jesus the man, the son of Mary. Jesus "came down from heaven" only in the way we all "came down from heaven"; he was conceived and born as we were conceived and born in the normal human way.

The Virgin Birth.

Was Jesus born of a virgin? The Christian tradition is very strong to the effect that Mary never had sexual intercourse. The Roman Catholic teaching is not only that Jesus was conceived without human sperm, but that he was born without breaking the virgin's hymen.[9] The scriptural evidence is not as clear as it might be. In Luke, Mary questioned the angel's proclamation that she will conceive a son, who will reign over the house of Jacob eternally, and said, "How can this be, since I am a virgin?" She may have been questioning the part about the eternal house of Jacob, but it is hard to see how she was questioning the possibility of conception, since she was engaged to Joseph and planning to be married soon. In Matthew's narrative, Joseph found out that Mary, to whom he was betrothed, was already pregnant when they had not yet made love, and he wanted to send her away in secret. If they were betrothed, how can Mary not have told Joseph of the visit of the angel Gabriel? Why did Joseph need an angel to tell him? And when Matthew and Luke each set forth the genealogy of Jesus, they both trace his line through Joseph, not through Mary. Had they forgotten so soon? But the tradition that Mary was always a virgin is strong.

I have four problems with accepting the virgin birth:

1.   It is unnecessary. The miracle of Jesus's conception was not that he was conceived with specially created and inseminated sperm; it was that his consciousness was wholly open to God. I don't see how the source of the sperm has anything to do with that. And if we believe that Jesus was truly human, his genetic material must have been a recombination of genetic material from a human mother and a human father, as is the case with all human beings.

2.   No one is benefited by the virgin birth. In nearly all the other miracles attributed to Jesus, someone is helped. The blind see, the lame walk, the hungry are fed, and so forth. But what good to anyone did the virgin birth do?

3.   The doctrine implies that virginity, or the celibate life, is inherently superior to married life and to normal human childbearing. This symbolically supports the Roman Stoic teachings that all sex acts not directly aimed at procreation are immoral, and even procreative sex acts are only barely permissible, as a concession to the flesh, views accepted by St. Augustine and through him by many Christian teachers through the ages.

4.   The symbolism of the virgin birth distances Jesus from the rest of humanity. It is critically important to the role of Jesus as redeemer that we have confidence that we can identify with him and follow his example. It is not helpful to be told that he is of human descent only on his mother's side. If Jesus had no human father, it becomes much easier to think of him as simply a god in disguise.

It thus seems to me that it is inconsistent with belief in the fully human nature of Jesus, and inconsistent with a sound view of human sexuality, to believe that his bodily conception was, or needed to be, out of the ordinary. So I view the virgin birth as a pious myth.

Miracles.

Did Jesus work miracles? The miracles of Jesus have been a serious problem for Christians for the last three centuries, as many enlightened and "scientific" thinkers have expressed their opinion that miracles could not have happened. Part of the problem is that some of the people who believe in Jesus's miracles are viewed as, and often are, credulous people. They tend to believe in saints and relics, and in the miracles of saints and the miraculous powers of relics. They often pray for miracles in their personal lives, and often they become convinced that miracles have occurred in their personal lives. This is in a way a magical rather than rational way of dealing with problems. Hence those who wish to conform to rational, modern and "scientific" ways of thought frequently feel they can simplify their view of the matter and purify their thinking from magical ways of thought by deciding that miracles cannot occur.

From the late seventeenth century through the early twentieth century, a commonly-held "scientific" view of the world was that the universal law of causality excludes any divine intervention in world events. Einstein wrote that "The man who is thoroughly convinced of the universal operation of the law of causation cannot for a moment entertain the idea of a being who interferes in the course of events."[10] I believe that there are several problems with this position:

1. It is no longer good science. According to quantum mechanics principles, the measured position of an electron cannot be absolutely determined; only the probability of its particular position can be determined. Its position does not flow from the law of causation, but from random probability. Modern physics thus holds that science cannot predict what result necessarily follows from a given cause; it can predict only the probability that a given result will follow. It follows from this that if God miraculously changed the result of a given cause from what the result otherwise would have been, but did not do so with measurable regularity, science *in principle* could not say whether or not a miraculous intervention had occurred. Einstein's cherished law of causation has been repeatedly and convincingly proved wrong in modern physics.[11]

2. The conviction that God cannot work miracles is

fundamentally not a scientific, but a philosophical, or theological, view of the world. It is not possible to demonstrate scientifically that God has never intervened in human affairs.

3. The argument from causality proves too much. If causality is truly universal, there is no room left for human free will or responsibility. So I have concluded that miracles may occur; whether any particular event is a miracle is another question.

Skepticism in the matter of miracles is a good thing. In general, as we saw in Chapter II, it seems to be God's plan for mankind that we must work to solve our problems, rather than pray that they go away. We should discover a cure for smallpox, or cancer, rather than simply pray that either disease not work its natural course. If we pray in the face of cancer, it should be for the dignity to bear it and the courage to fight it. And we must acknowledge that the possibility of a miraculous cure in answer to prayer is very small. Yet excessive skepticism— unwillingness to examine the evidence with an open mind, or the construction of exceedingly improbable rationalizations to "explain away" the evidence—must also be avoided. C. S. Lewis described such excessive skepticism as follows:

> "The ordinary procedure of the modern historian, even if he admits the possibility of a miracle, is to admit no particular instance of it until every possibility of 'natural' explanation has been tried and failed. That is, he will accept the most improbable 'natural' explanations rather than say that a miracle occurred. Collective hallucination, hypnotism of unconsenting spectators, widespread instantaneous conspiracy in lying by persons not otherwise known to be liars and not likely to gain by the lie—all these are known to be very improbable events: so improbable that, except for the special purpose of excluding a miracle, they are never suggested. But they are preferred to the admission of a miracle."[12]

Science and reason cannot conclude that miracles cannot be performed. Skeptical analysis can help us sort out the true miracles from the false, but it cannot conclude that none have occurred. As yet unexplained data is always a problem for the scientist, but there is a fair amount of unexplained data in every scientific field.

Jesus is reported as having performed many miracles, and he said frequently that he did so with power given him by his Father, to convince his listeners that his teaching was true. For some, though not all, of the miracles narrated in the Gospels, the evangelists show reasonable skepticism by taking pains to show that the miracle was tested by rational means. For example, when Jesus healed a leper (Mt 8, 1), he commanded the leper to go show himself to the priest. When he healed the centurion's palsied servant (Mt 8, 5), he did so without ever seeing the servant, thus ruling out any possibility of hypnotic suggestion or hysterical reaction to his presence. He raised the daughter of Jairus from death (Mk 5, 22) after the servants of Jairus had independently confirmed her death. The Pharisees diligently and skeptically inquired of the man born blind whom Jesus restored to sight (Jn 9, 3), and of his parents; and so forth. There is no reason for believing that people were less skeptical or more credulous in the first century than they are now. Human nature hasn't changed much in the last two thousand years, and the Pharisees were no friends of Jesus.

Jesus is unique. He is the only human who was gifted with full God-consciousness from the moment of his conception. There is no "scientific" way of knowing what powers would naturally accompany this full God-consciousness. As a scientist would say, "It is very difficult to do statistics with an N of one."[13] All the evidence we have which shows us the powers of a person with a fully-developed God-consciousness, of whom there is one such example, shows us that he could heal the sick, feed the multitudes, and raise the dead to life. In my view, it is unscientific to conclude *a priori* that this evidence is false. I accept one miracle, which is God's endowment of Jesus with the power of full God-consciousness, and then I find that this power, in the single case in which it occurred, was accompanied by the powers to heal the sick, feed the multitudes and raise the dead. The miracles of Jesus are not supernatural acts, but simply natural exercises of his natural but unique powers.

Jesus's Description of His Powers.

Jesus's public ministry began, in the narrations of Matthew, Mark and Luke, with his baptism by John the Baptist, and this was immediately followed by the temptations in the desert. The story of the temptations of Jesus by the devil is a strange one; many people have been puzzled by it, and have not seen that it has a point, or what that point might be. It seems to me that in this story Jesus is telling us how it felt to him to have a growing personal consciousness of his unique relationship with God in him and of the singular powers which accompanied that relationship. As we look at the narration, we should bear in mind that, in contrast to most of the events narrated in the Gospels, no one was present to witness the temptations in the desert except Jesus himself. Thus this must be a story which Jesus himself told his disciples. We should also remember that Jesus frequently expressed himself in parables, and that often his disciples did not understand the parables. Sometimes they asked him to explain a parable, and he did so. Sometimes they didn't ask. Sometimes they did not even grasp that the teaching was a parable. This is the case with the story of the temptations in the desert.

Jesus had fasted for forty days, and he was hungry. "The tempter came and said to him, 'If you are the Son of God, command these stones to become loaves of bread.'" Mt 4, 3. What Jesus is saying is that he realized that, with his powers, he could fully satisfy his physical needs and desires; he could live in comfort and plenty and would never have to work; he could be a man of wealth and ease. He rejected this option. "Then the devil took him to the holy city and placed him on the pinnacle of the temple, saying to him, 'If you are the Son of

God, throw yourself down . . . . '" Mt 4, 6. Jesus is telling us that he knew he could use his powers to amaze men; he could achieve celebrity, fame and the adulation of the masses; he could be a superstar. He rejected this use of his powers. "Again, the devil took him to a very high mountain and showed him all the kingdoms of the world and their splendor, and he said to him, 'All these I will give you, if you will fall down and worship me.'" Mt 4, 9. Jesus realized that, with his powers, he could rule the world. He rejected this alternative. "Then the devil left him." Mt 4, 11.

So Matthew and Luke have here recorded Jesus's own testimony (a) that he possessed extraordinary powers which were not conditioned on his proper use of them, but which were his to use or abuse as he chose; (b) that he was fully aware that with these powers he could obtain wealth, fame, and the power to rule over men; and (c) that he instead chose to do "the will of him who sent me," knowing, as he did, how that would probably end up. Jesus was not an automaton, nor a simple "mouthpiece" for God. He was a uniquely gifted but very human person who realized what he was and what he had. He knew that his powers were sufficient to obtain wealth, fame and power for himself, if he forsook his mission. He nevertheless knowingly and deliberately chose to pursue his mission.

As I mentioned earlier, some writers have suggested that parts of the Gospels are not narrations of what took place and what Jesus said, but are inventions of the second generation of Christians, intended to meet the needs of their new local Christian communities. This is inherently implausible, because the core teachings of Jesus are generally so different and so difficult, so creatively and brilliantly expressed, and so internally consistent, as to make it wholly unlikely that later writers could have made them up. It is even more implausible to suggest that later writers would invent narratives which they obviously did not themselves understand. Such narratives could not possibly have been thought by these writers to be responsive to the needs of their communities, or to be responsive to anything at all. The story of the temptations in the desert is one, but not the only, example of a narrative which could not have been invented, because the writers who wrote it down appear to have had no idea what it meant or was intended to mean. Its appearance in the Gospels is consistent only with the view that the evangelists simply put down what they had been told Jesus had said, whether they understood it or not, just because Jesus had said it.

Gifted with his unique and extraordinary consciousness of God, and with the accompanying power to work miracles, Jesus lived in almost total obscurity until he was about thirty years old. He then began his public life of teaching and healing, which is recorded in the Gospels. We turn now to give close attention to what Jesus said.

Notes:

1. See Brown, Raymond E., *An Introduction to the New Testament* (Doubleday, 1997).
2. Crossan, John D., *The Historical Jesus* (Harper-Collins, 1991), p. xxix.
3. Miller, Robert J., ed., *The Complete Gospels* (Polebridge Press, 1994), pp. 307, 314.
4. Cahill, Thomas, *Desire of the Everlasting Hills* (Talese/Anchor Books, 2001), p. 284.
5. Mayr, Ernst, *What Evolution Is* (Basic Books, 2001), pp. 74, 83.
6. Bloesch, Donald G., *Essentials of Evangelical Theology*, Vol. 1 (Harper-Collins, 1982), p. 129 (Emphasis added).
7. Schleiermacher, Friedrich, *The Christian Faith* (Harper Torchbooks, 1963), Sections 89-100; *The Life of Jesus* (Fortress Press, 1975).
8. Alison, James, *Raising Abel* (Crossroad Publishing Co., 1996), p. 40.
9. *Catechism of the Catholic Church* (Doubleday Image Books, 1995), Sections 496, 499.
10. Calaprice, Alice, ed., *The Expanded Quotable Einstein* (Princeton University Press, 2000), pp. 205-06.

11. See, e.g., Greene, Brian, *The Elegant Universe* (Vintage Books, 2000), pp. 107-08.
12. Lewis, C. S., *Miracles, a Preliminary Study* (MacMillan Company, 1947), pp. 103-04.
13. Ward, Peter and Brownlee, Donald, *Rare Earth; Why Complex Life Is Uncommon in the Universe* (Copernicus, 2000), p. ix.

V

The Teachings of Jesus.

We can discover the mission of Jesus from an examination of his teachings as recorded in the Gospels. When we look to the Gospels and read Jesus's teachings, what do we find? The first thing we find is that they are not organized. They are not grouped by subject matter. Some teachings occur only once; others are repeated, or expanded, but in no discernable order. It is hard to see themes and patterns. The writers of the Gospels apparently thought that what they would do is record the teachings as they had heard them and let their readers make whatever analysis or organization they thought appropriate. (In a way, their concentration on recording the original words of Jesus rather than their own analysis gives us another reason to trust them as accurate recorders of his words.)

While all of Jesus's teachings are significant in some way, they are not all of equal importance. I have studied the teachings to see if an organizing pattern emerges from the body of Jesus's sayings, and I find that it does. First, there is a valid and useful distinction which can be made between the central or core teachings of Jesus and those of his teachings which are peripheral or occasional. Second, the core teachings themselves can be organized by subject matter. When they are so organized, they reveal a central theme. From this central theme we can discover why Jesus came and what his mission was.

I propose to discuss the teachings of Jesus in this way: First, I consider the fact that many people do not think the teachings of Jesus are a really important part of his mission. Second, I distinguish between Jesus's peripheral teachings and his central or core teachings. Third, I set forth the core teachings of Jesus in his own words, but in an organized fashion.

How Important Are Jesus's Teachings?

There seems to be a real question among Christians whether the teachings of Jesus are truly important. We all agree that they are good, and beautiful, and inspiring. But so are the teachings of the Hebrew prophets and those of many other holy men and women. In many ways, Jesus's teachings have not been, and are not now, generally treated as being of central significance to his mission.

While the Gospels are full of Jesus's teachings, the rest of the New Testament makes very little reference to them. In the Acts of the Apostles, the apostles worked miracles and preached the resurrection of Jesus, not his teachings. The death and resurrection of Jesus is the center of the teaching of St. Paul, and he picked up and developed Jesus's teachings about the differences between the old covenant and the new. He did teach what I call the key virtues (see Chapter VIII), but there is nowhere in Paul's writings or those of any of the other writers of epistles any detailed description or exposition of the teachings of Jesus as such.

Both the words of the Apostles' Creed and those of the Nicene Creed proceed directly from Jesus's birth to his death without any reference to his teachings. Does this indicate that Jesus's teachings were without doctrinal significance in the early Christian church?

In the course of preparing this writing, I have looked into a number of books on various theological subjects, and I have been surprised to find in them so much about Jesus, and so little about what he actually taught. For example, Alister McGrath's excellent and thorough *Christian Theology: An Introduction*,[1] one of the leading current textbooks in Christian theology, says, in over 600 pages, virtually nothing about the teachings of Jesus. In her *A History of God*,[2] Karen Armstrong gives no attention whatever to the teachings of Jesus on the loving kindness of his Father. Joseph Kelly's *The Problem of Evil in the Western Tradition*[3] is a survey of how evil has been understood in the West from the biblical era until today. Kelly gives three pages to the thoughts of Origen, and eleven to Augustine, but says nothing about any teachings of Jesus. Does he believe that Jesus had nothing new or interesting to say about evil? In his best-selling *Desire of the Everlasting Hills*,[4] Thomas Cahill describes a fundamental continuity of ethical teaching (as he sees it) from the Jewish prophets to Jesus. In Cahill's view, Jesus's teachings were not essentially new.

I take a quite different view, which I will explain below. But first it will be helpful to look at some of the reasons why the teachings of Jesus have been ignored, or set off to one side, when it comes to talking about his redemptive mission.

If, as Anselm's explanation has it, the central mission of Jesus was to offer his life to God as a perfect sacrifice, to make substitutionary atonement for the sins of mankind, and thus to reunite mankind with God, his teaching ministry would not be an essential part of that mission. The principal function of his teaching activity would be to give him public exposure and notoriety, and to anger and inflame the leaders of the Jews, so that they would be properly motivated to carry out their part in causing his sacrificial execution. (I will explain the true relationship of Jesus's teachings to his death in Chapter VII.)

Many writers have taken the view, as Cahill does, that Jesus's teachings consisted substantially of repeating the standard morality of the prophets and of the Old Testament, although perhaps at a higher level and certainly very beautifully. There was nothing new and different about the first and second commandments: "Jesus said, 'You must love the Lord your God with all your heart, with all your soul, and with all your mind. This is the greatest and the first commandment. The second resembles it: You must love your neighbor as yourself.'" Mt 22, 37-39. Nor is there anything new about the golden rule: "In everything do to others as you would have them do to you; for this is the law and the prophets." Mt 7, 12. Both of these were contained in the Old Testament. Deut 6, 5; Lev 19, 18; Tob 4, 15. Most authors will admit that Jesus's metaphors and parables were brilliantly creative. But he never pulled his teachings together in an organized fashion which would clearly show that he had a new revelation and a new program in mind.

The teachings of Jesus are certainly given a major role in Christian worship services. A portion of the Gospels is read every Sunday at every Christian service, and Gospel texts are often used as the subject of the sermon. But there is a separation in Christian theology and in Christian seminary training between dogmatic or doctrinal theology on the one hand and pastoral or ethical theology on the other hand, a separation which goes back to the days of very early Christianity. It seems to me that the dogmatic theologians have simply conceded the teachings of Jesus to the pastoral theologians, and have not considered their doctrinal implications.

I find that Jesus himself expressed a quite contrary view, and I believe that we should listen to him. Jesus himself repeatedly said that his teaching was what he came to do, and that salvation would come from his teaching. Jesus said, "I must proclaim the Good News of the kingdom of God to the other towns too, because *that is what I was sent to do.*" Lk 4, 43. "For this I was born, and for this I came into the world, to testify to the truth." Jn 18, 37. "The words that I have spoken to you are spirit and life." Jn 6, 63. "If you continue in my word, you are truly my disciples; and you will know the truth, and the truth will make you free." Jn 8, 31. "Whoever keeps my word will never see death." Jn 8, 51. In Jesus's own words, his teaching activity is why he was born, and what he was sent to do, and those who accept his teachings and follow them will be redeemed.

The Core Teachings and
the Peripheral Teachings.

In studying the teachings of Jesus, I have found that there is a valid and helpful distinction which may be made between his core teachings and his peripheral teachings. Here is what I see as the differences between them:

One key indicator that a particular teaching is part of the core teachings is that Jesus repeatedly taught it. A teaching which appears only once or twice in the Gospels is a peripheral teaching. Since the golden rule appears only once in the Gospels (Mt 7,12), I do not consider it a core teaching of Jesus. Similarly, Jesus's injunction against looking on a woman with lust (Mt 5, 27) is not repeated elsewhere in the Gospels. This saying can be taken as another illustration of Jesus's fundamental and core teaching that the center of ethical conduct must be moved from the external act to the internal disposition, but it is not a core teaching itself.

Another key indicator that a teaching of Jesus is part of his core teaching is that it appears in the "stump speech." As anyone who has listened to itinerant lecturers or politicians knows, the basic speech, which I call the "stump speech," is what the speaker came to say. What comes up in the question and answer period following the speech is what the audience is curious about. The answers may be important, or revealing, but they are not part of the basic message of the speaker. Jesus was an itinerant preacher for some time, and he must have had a "stump speech." To be sure, Jesus said many important and revealing things in answers to questions. I do not belittle them, but I do not believe that they were part of his core, new and unique teachings.

The two great commandments are stated only in answer to a question put by a scribe to test Jesus (Mt 22, 34-40; Mk 12, 28-31). In Luke's narration, they are recited not by Jesus but by the questioner (Lk 10, 25-28). Similarly, the only reference to the ten commandments in Jesus's teachings is his first answer to the rich man who turned away: "You know the commandments: you shall not murder; you shall not commit adultery; you shall not steal; you shall not bear false witness; you shall not defraud;

honor your father and mother." Mk 10, 19; Mt 19, 18; Lk 18, 20. (Notice that Jesus said nothing about keeping holy the Sabbath day.) The story of the rich man goes on to make another point entirely, how hard it is for a rich man to enter the kingdom of heaven, which is a core teaching of Jesus. Jesus's teaching on the indissolubility of marriage, "What God has joined together, let no man put asunder," Mt 19, 6; Mk 10, 9, was given in answer to questions from the Pharisees. I do not think that there is any teaching of Jesus on human sexual conduct which qualifies as a core teaching.

Jesus did not teach the duty of performing charitable works, the corporal works of mercy, as part of his core teaching. He mentioned them only in passing. He several times called on people to sell their goods and give to the poor. Lk 6, 38; Lk 12, 33. It was from such a call that the rich man in the story above turned away. The only place where the corporal works of mercy (feed the hungry, give drink to the thirsty, shelter the stranger, clothe the naked, care for the sick, visit the imprisoned) are listed in the Gospels is in the story of the last judgment, in Matthew's Gospel alone. Mt 25, 31-46. There is the story of the Good Samaritan (Lk 10, 29-37), and there is the healing work of Jesus's miracles; but no further teaching on charitable works. This is not to say that the two great commandments and the performance of charitable works are unimportant. But they are part of the natural law, which humans already knew. No new revelation of them was needed, so they are not really a part of the core teachings of Jesus.

In Chapter II, I set forth my understanding of the economy of God's ways toward humanity. As I there concluded, God generally intends people to figure things out for themselves. God has not provided guidance to humans on most moral or intellectual questions, so that men and women would remain free to work out the answers with their own collective intelligence and judgment. In the areas without divine guidance, men and women are free, even if the price of freedom is centuries or millennia of error and human suffering. If, as I described in Chapter

IV, Jesus was in constant communion with God, through his absolute facility in consciousness of God, he would observe God's economy. I believe he did so. Thus the core teachings of Jesus do not set forth answers to questions humans can solve without divine guidance.

A striking characteristic of Jesus's teachings is the fact that he taught only about the Kingdom of God, its ethical constitution, its relation to the Father, and his own relation to the Kingdom and to the Father. He said nothing about politics. "Render to Caesar the things which are Caesar's" tells us nothing about how civil society should be organized. He said nothing about slavery, although slavery was widely practiced in his time. He said nothing about economics, except to say frequently that it would be harder for rich people to enter the Kingdom than it would be for poor people. He said nothing about literature, music, or the arts. He said nothing about how his church should be organized or governed, except to indicate that Peter should assume a leadership role after his death. He set forth few moral rules. He welcomed the company of prostitutes, tax collectors and other sinners or criminals, and he did not inveigh against their sins. Lk 15, 3. He never spoke of birth control, abortion, homosexuality, public indecency, or other moral and ethical issues involving sexuality. He never spoke of family values. Indeed, he was rather callously indifferent to his own family and relatives (Mk 3, 31-35; Lk 8, 19-21). We remain without guidance from Jesus in nearly all matters of politics, economics, and family values, and in the organization and governance of the Christian churches.

If Jesus did teach something as part of his core teachings, it is almost certainly (a) something which men and women would not have been able to work out on their own, or (b) something which runs so counter to the natural urges and inclinations of men and women that people would almost certainly reject it unless Jesus really insisted upon it.

An example of the former is Jesus's teaching that God is our Father, who cares for us and loves us. This is wholly non-obvious, and it was hidden from mankind until Jesus taught it. The God of the Greek and Christian philosophers is completely "other" and inexpressibly distant from man. The God of the Old Testament is most of the time a wrathful, vengeful, tribal God. The pagan gods of the culture of sacrifice were, in turns, wrathful, callous, or unconcerned with men and women, but never loving and caring.

An example of the latter is Jesus's teaching that we must cultivate the attitude of true interior humility. That runs so strongly against our natural inclinations that most people reject it, and many of us who do take it seriously can become proud and self-satisfied with our own humility. As Pascal observed:

> "Vanity is so anchored in the heart of man that a soldier, a soldier's servant, a cook, a porter brags, and wishes to have his admirers. Even philosophers wish for them. Those who write against it want to have the glory of having written well; and those who read it desire the glory of having read it. I who write this have perhaps this desire, and perhaps those who will read it . . . ."[5]

The Core Teachings of Jesus.

I have found that Jesus's core teachings can be organized under four major headings: (a) The Key Virtues; (b) Rules, Rituals, Practices and Prayer; (c) God, the Kingdom and the Role of Jesus; and (d) The Great Promises. We begin with the key virtues.

a.   The Key Virtues.

Jesus began his public teaching ministry with the words, "Repent, for the kingdom of heaven has come near." Mt 4, 17; Mk 1, 15. The Greek word that is translated as "repent" is *metanoeite*, which does not mean "repent." It literally means "change your minds." The core of Jesus's moral teaching is his call to men and women to change their minds in five very specific ways. In each one, the call is to act contrary to a behavior pattern imprinted in the human genome by natural selection, and to tear down the formidable psychological defenses we all have erected against acting contrary to these primal instincts. These teachings are non-obvious. They are new and different. They are very difficult to follow. The five specific virtues commanded by Jesus are non-violence, non-judging, forgiveness, interior humility, and detachment from possessions. Jesus called for these virtues again and again, and illustrated each with examples and parables which make his teachings absolutely clear. Let us take them one by one, in the words of Jesus.

The first three key virtues, non-violence, non-judging and forgiveness, form a group which I call the "external virtues," because they set forth what must become our habitual responses to the conduct of other people.

Non-Violence. In the Sermon on the Mount, Jesus said, "Blessed are the merciful, for they will receive mercy." Mt 5, 7. "Blessed are the peacemakers, for they will be called children of God." Mt 5, 9. "But I say to you that if you are angry with a brother or sister, you will be liable to judgment; and if you insult a brother or sister, you will be liable to the council; and if you say 'You fool,' you will be liable to the hell of fire." Mt 5, 22. Jesus said,

> "You have heard that it was said, 'An eye for an eye and a tooth for a tooth.' But I say to you, Do not resist an evildoer. But if anyone strikes you on the right cheek, turn the other also; and if anyone wants to sue you and take your coat, give your cloak as well; and if anyone forces you to go one mile, go also the second mile. . . . Love your enemies and pray for those who persecute you, so that you may be children of your Father in heaven." Mt 5, 38-41, 44; Lk 6, 27-29.

And when Jesus was taken in the garden, and a disciple drew his sword, Jesus said, "Put your sword back into its place, for all who take the sword will perish by the sword." Mt 26, 52.

Non-violence, to Jesus, is absolute and without exception. Leo Tolstoy expressed it this way: "Why had I always sought for some ulterior motive? 'Do not resist an evildoer' means *never* resist, *never* oppose violence; or, in other words, never do anything contrary to the law of love."[6]

Non-Judging. Again from the Sermon on the Mount, Jesus said,

> "Do not judge, and you will not be judged, because the judgments you give are the judgments you will get, and the amount you measure out is the amount you will be given. Why do you observe the mote in your brother's eye and never notice the beam in your own? How dare you say to your brother, 'Let me take the mote out of your eye,' when all the time there is a beam in your own? Hypocrite! Take the beam out of your own eye first, and then you will see clearly enough to take the mote out of your brother's eye." Mt 7, 1-5; Lk 6, 37, 41-42.

When the scribes and Pharisees brought to Jesus a woman who had been caught in adultery, and asked him to approve their stoning her to death, as the law prescribed, Jesus replied, "Let him who is without sin cast the first stone." And they went away, one by one. Jesus said to her, "'Woman, where are they? Has no one condemned you?' She said, 'No one, sir.' And Jesus said, 'Neither do I condemn you. Go your way, and from now on do not sin again.'" Jn 8, 1-11.

Judging, as Jesus uses the word in this teaching, does not mean determining with one's conscience whether an act is wise or foolish, or good or evil, but (a) transferring blame to another for one's own troubles, or (b) deciding that the other should be punished or excluded for his or her fault, or (c) determining that it is allowable to inflict violence on the other for his or her fault. René Girard points out, in *The Scapegoat*, that "*Crisis, crime, criteria, critique*, all share a common root in the Greek work *krino*, which means not only to judge, distinguish, differentiate, but also *to accuse and condemn a victim*."[7] What Jesus condemned was both (i) exaggerating the fault of the other and minimizing or ignoring one's own fault (the mote and the beam), and (ii) even where the other's fault is clear, taking or approving punitive or violent action against the offender (the woman caught in adultery). The correct but counter-instinctive action in both cases, Jesus taught, is an acute consciousness of one's own failings, followed by forgiveness of the other person grounded in love.

Wrongful judging, in Jesus's teachings, also includes judging another person inferior, blameworthy or an enemy because that person is of a different ethnic or religious group:

> "A man was going down from Jerusalem to Jericho, and fell into the hands of robbers, who stripped him, beat him, and went away, leaving him half-dead. Now by chance a priest was going down that road; and when he saw him, he passed by on the other side. So likewise a Levite, when he came to the place and saw him, passed by on the other side. But a Samaritan while traveling came near him; and when he saw him, he was moved with pity. He went to him and bandaged his wounds, having poured oil and wine on them. Then he put him on his own animal, brought him to an inn, and took care of him. The next day he took out two denarii, gave them to the innkeeper, and said, 'Take care of him; and when I come back, I will repay you whatever more you spend.' Which of these three, do you think, was a neighbor to the man who fell into the hands of these robbers?" He said, "The one who showed him mercy." Jesus said to him, "Go and do likewise." Lk 10, 30-37.

This parable is a lesson in brotherly love, but it is also a lesson in non-judging. The priest and the Levite were Jews, but of a certain class. They obviously considered themselves superior to the victim and avoided him. The Samaritan was of a different ethnic and religious group, shunned by the Jews, but he did not judge the wounded Jew unworthy of his pity and care.

When I first began to sort out and classify the teachings of

Jesus, to determine which teachings he repeatedly taught, I was frankly surprised to see non-judging emerge as a key virtue. Non-violence I expected, and forgiveness, humility and detachment from possessions were obviously key virtues. But non-judging? At first it seemed to me that getting along with people who are different from you or me is part of everyday living. Not blaming others for one's own fault is part of developing an ordinary mature sense of responsibility. And not calling to another's attention the problems you have with his or her conduct is just normal good manners. I could not understand why Jesus was making such a big thing out of non-judging, out of the mote and the beam. It seemed to me that he was just making a beam out of a mote.

I was greatly mistaken. If there is a key to the key virtues, non-judging is the key. Jesus was talking about collective as well as individual sins; sins which begin with an individual but spread contagiously within a group. Judging, which is highly contagious, is the individual and collective act of identifying someone (or some other group) as not "one of us," and therefore not deserving of the respect and protection we accord to those who are "one of us," members of the group. Judging of this kind precedes every act of violence (as well as every act of dominant or hierarchical behavior). For nearly all of us, it is necessary to believe that the victim is unlike ourselves, and is blameworthy and deserving of expulsion, punishment or death, before we are able to expel or inflict violence on him or her. Judging, in this sense, is the way the human sacrifice works: the victim is excluded from the tribe, the community transfers its blame and guilt to the victim, and only then can the victim be sacrificed. Nothing is so contagious within a group, and so unites a group, as collective judging, identifying and excluding the outsider or the enemy.

Excluding the outsider, the stranger, the Other (for Christians through history, the heretic, the Muslim and the Jew), and persuading ourselves in our own minds that this is the right and normal way of organizing our lives and our communities, is so common for us that I failed to see that this is exactly what Jesus was condemning. He rightly saw that non-judging runs against our instinctive behavior, our genetically-based kinship affinity. Jesus was calling for a revolution in our genetically-based ways of thinking about and classifying other people. Jesus was telling us that God's way is different. As James Alison puts it, "For God there are no 'outsiders,' which means that *any mechanism for the creation of outsiders is automatically and simply a mechanism of human violence,* and that's that."[8]

Forgiveness. I take Jesus's calls for forgiveness as a continuation and reinforcement of the virtues of non-violence and non-judging. The three operate together. The follower of Jesus's teachings represses the urge to retaliate with violence for an insult or injury. She makes allowance for the fault of the person giving the injury, and reflects on the beam in her own eye. Then she puts the matter at peace within herself and puts it behind her when she forgives the other person. In Luke, Jesus connects these virtues this way: "Do not judge, and you will not be judged; do not condemn, and you will not be condemned; forgive, and you will be forgiven." Lk 6, 37.

In the Lord's Prayer, Jesus tells us to pray, "Forgive us our trespasses, as we forgive those who trespass against us." Mt 6, 12; Lk 11, 4; Mk 11, 25. "Then Peter came and said to him, 'Lord, if my brother sins against me, how often shall I forgive? As often as seven times?' Jesus said to him, 'Not seven times, but, I tell you, seventy times seven.'" Mt 18, 21-22. Jesus immediately followed this saying by telling the parable of the unjust debtor, who, after the king had forgiven him his large and unpayable debt, refused to forgive the debt of another servant who owed him a very small amount, and had his debtor thrown into debtor's prison. When the king learned of it, he seized the unforgiving debtor and handed him over to the torturers. Jesus concluded, "So my heavenly Father will also do to every one of you, if you do not forgive your brother or sister from your heart." Mt 18, 23-39. Jesus taught that his Father is willing, even eager, to forgive, in the parable of the Prodigal Son, Lk 15, 11-32.

The next two virtues, humility and detachment from

possessions, form a group which I call the "internal virtues," because they do not relate to control of our responses to others, but to control of our own pride and acquisitiveness.

Humility. Jesus said, "Blessed are the meek, for they will inherit the earth." Mt 5, 5. "Whenever you give alms, do not sound a trumpet before you, as the hypocrites do . . . . Truly I tell you, they have received their reward. But when you give alms, do not let your left hand know what your right hand is doing, so that your alms may be done in secret; and your Father who sees in secret will reward you." Mt 6, 2-4. Similarly, pray in secret, and fast in secret. Mt 6, 5-6, 16-18.

Some of Jesus's teaching is psychologically very astute. He suggests that if you are having a hard time being humble, use your pride and your fear of public humiliation to develop the habit of acting humbly:

> "When you are invited by someone to a wedding banquet, do not sit down at the place of honor, in case someone more distinguished than you has been invited by your host; and the host who invited both of you may come and say to you, 'Give this person your place,' and then in disgrace you would start to take the lowest place. But when you are invited, go and sit down at the lowest place, so that when your host comes, he may say to you, 'Friend, move up higher'; then you will be honored in the presence of all who sit at the table with you. For all who exalt themselves will be humbled, and those who humble themselves will be exalted." Lk 14, 8-11.

Jesus said, "Whoever wishes to be great among you must be your servant . . . just as the Son of Man came not to be served but to serve." Mt 20, 26-28; Mk 10, 43-45; Lk 22, 26-27. As a sign of this, Jesus washed the feet of his disciples at the Last Supper. Jn 13, 3-17. And he told this parable:

"Two men went up to the temple to pray, one a Pharisee and the other a tax collector. The Pharisee, standing by himself, was praying thus, 'God, I thank you that I am not like other people: thieves, rogues, adulterers, or even like this tax collector. I fast twice a week; I give a tenth of all my income.' But the tax collector, standing far off, would not even look up to heaven, but was beating his breast and saying, 'God, be merciful to me, a sinner.' I tell you, this man went down to his home justified rather than the other; for all who exalt themselves will be humbled, but all who humble themselves will be exalted." Lk 18, 10-14.

Jesus specifically instructed his disciples that there are to be no hierarchies, no dominant-submissive relationships, among his followers: "You are not to be called rabbi, for you have one teacher, and you are all students. And call no one your father on earth, for you have one Father—the one in heaven. Nor are you to be called instructors, for you have one instructor, the Messiah." Mt 23, 8-10. How could he have said more clearly that, in the Kingdom, all men and women are created equal, with all the revolutionary implications of that statement?

Detachment from Possessions. Jesus said, "Blessed are the poor in spirit, for theirs is the kingdom of heaven." Mt 5, 3; Lk 6, 20. "No one can be the slave of two masters . . . . You cannot be the slave both of God and of money." Mt 6, 24; Lk 16, 13. Jesus said,

"Do not worry about your life, what you will eat or what you will drink, or about your body, what you will wear. . . . Look at the birds of the air; they neither sow nor reap nor gather into barns, and yet your heavenly Father feeds them . . . . Consider the lilies of the field, how they grow; they neither toil nor spin, yet I tell you even Solomon in all his glory was not clothed like one of these. But if God so clothes the grass of the field, which is alive today and tomorrow is thrown into the oven, will he not much more clothe you—you of little faith?" Mt 6, 25-30; Lk 12, 22-31.

Jesus also said, "It is easier for a camel to pass through the eye of a needle than for a rich man to enter the kingdom of heaven." Mt 19, 24; Mk 10, 25; Lk 18, 25. "Be on your guard against all kinds of greed; for one's life does not consist in an abundance of possessions." Lk 12, 15. "Where your treasure is, there your heart will be also." Lk 12, 34. "None of you can become my disciple if you do not give up all your possessions." Lk 14, 33.

Reflections on the Key Virtues. The key virtues taught by Jesus are difficult to accept and more difficult to master; much more so than obeying the ten commandments and living the ordinary good, hard-working, respectable life which most of us do without much difficulty most of the time. This is because each of these key virtues runs directly counter to a genetically-based behavior inherited by humans from our animal ancestors.

Take the external virtues. If we are attacked or threatened with attack, the normal and instinctive human response, contained in our genes, is to answer with violence, reciprocal violence. We consider ourselves virtuous if our violence is no more than proportional to the attack, that is, it is imitative: "An eye for an eye, a tooth for a tooth." This primal human instinct to respond to violence with greater violence is the center and source of the culture of sacrifice described in Chapter III. If we are insulted or threatened, our normal and primal response is to judge the hostile party to be worthy of blame and guilty of ignorance or malice or both. Non-violence and withholding of judgment are not natural to us. Deep down, we feel they are dangerous to us, because they will expose us to harm. As for forgiveness, our natural survival instinct is to incapacitate the enemy first, then forgive him.

The same is true of the internal virtues; they seem unnatural. We value and try to develop self-esteem. We think it normal and admirable to strive for status, and to be honored for achievements. We fear that if we don't seek to dominate, we will be forced to submit. This behavior is partially genetic, as is our constant striving for acquisition of possessions, and our tendency to find our own self-worth in the quantity and quality of our things.

There are ascetic and monastic traditions in the far East which try to live by these anti-instinctive virtues, but I think that only in the teachings of Jesus are they set forth as the standards to which all men and women are called. Jesus is calling for a fundamental change in the psychology of humanity, and a resulting fundamental change in human society. I suggest, and will develop further in what follows, that accomplishing this fundamental change is nothing less than the second half of God's creation of humanity. I think that so completing the creation of humanity is what Jesus was referring to when he said, "My food is to do the will of him who sent me *and to complete his work.*" Jn 4, 34.

b.   Rules, Rituals, Practices and Prayer.

Jesus delivered an extended and systematic attack on the rules, rituals and practices of Judaism, and taught that those practices should be replaced by private prayer.

Sabbath Observance. Jesus went out of his way to flout the rules of observance of the Sabbath as then taught and practiced in Israel. He deliberately incurred the anger and hostility of the scribes and Pharisees in doing so. On one occasion, Jesus and his disciples were in a grainfield on the Sabbath, and his disciples, being hungry, plucked the grain and ate it. The Pharisees told Jesus that what his disciples were doing was not lawful on the Sabbath. Jesus defended his disciples, cited precedent in the law, and concluded by saying, "The Sabbath was made for mankind, and not mankind for the Sabbath; so the Son of Man is Lord even of the Sabbath." Mk 2, 23-28; Mt 12, 1-8; Lk 6, 1-5.

Jesus performed no fewer than five miracles of healing on the Sabbath, in each case in the face of the opposition and hostility of the Jewish religious establishment: a man with a withered hand, Mk 3, 1-6; Mt 12, 9-14; Lk 6, 6-11; a woman who had been crippled for eighteen years, Lk 13, 10-17; a man with dropsy, Lk 14, 1-6; a man who had been an invalid for thirty-eight years, Jn 5, 2-18; and a man born blind, Jn 9, 1-41. Preceding two of these cures, he challenged the observing Pharisees, asking whether it was lawful to cure on the Sabbath. On both occasions his question was met with stony silence. In all five of the cases the Jewish religious leaders subsequently condemned his actions. In two of the cases it is reported that they then plotted to kill him.

Ritual and Dietary Cleanness. Jesus regularly defied the Jewish rules of ritual cleanness. The scribes and Pharisees asked him why his disciples broke ritual cleanness by eating with unwashed hands. He answered with an angry attack on their practice of *Corban*, by which one could avoid the responsibility for supporting an aged parent by offering the support money to the temple. He called them hypocrites, said they were the blind leading the blind. Jesus was invited to dinner on one occasion by a Pharisee, who rather discourteously observed that Jesus did not wash before dinner. Jesus replied to him, with equal discourtesy, "Oh, you Pharisees! You clean the outside of cup and plate, while inside yourselves you are filled with extortion and wickedness." Lk 11, 37-42; Mt 23, 25.

Jesus certainly knew the second chapter of Genesis, where "the Lord God commanded the man, 'You may freely eat of every tree of the garden; but of the tree of the knowledge of good and evil you shall not eat, for in the day that you eat of it you shall die.'" Gen 2, 16-17. But Jesus preached that "What goes into the mouth does not make a man unclean; it is what comes out of the mouth which makes him unclean." Mt 15, 10-20; Mk 7, 14-23. As the author of Mark observes, "Thus he pronounced all foods clean." Mk 7, 19.

Jesus criticized the scribes and Pharisees for placing ritual practices above the law of God:

> "You hypocrites, it was a true prophecy Isaiah made of you, writing as he did, This people does me honor with their lips, but its heart is far from me; their worship of me is vain, for the doctrines they teach are the commandments of men. You leave God's commandments on one side, and hold to the tradition of man, the purifying of pitchers and cups, and many other like observances. And he told them,

> You have quite defeated God's commandment, to establish
> your own tradition instead." Mk 7, 6-9.

And he denounced the religious leaders generally for the multitude of little rules and ritual observances which they taught and enforced, all in the name of Jewish law and tradition: "Alas for you, scribes and Pharisees, you hypocrites! You who pay your tithe of mint and dill and cummin and have neglected the weightier matters of the Law—justice, mercy, good faith! These you should have practiced, without neglecting the others. You blind guides! Straining out gnats and swallowing camels!" Mt 23, 23-24; Lk 11, 42.

Sacrifice. Jesus attacked the central practice of sacrifice. The Pharisees had criticized Jesus to his disciples, saying "Why does your master eat with tax collectors and sinners?" Jesus answered, "Go and learn the meaning of the words: 'What I want is mercy, not sacrifice.' And indeed I did not come to call the virtuous, but sinners." Mt 9, 10-13. He said it again, defending his disciples for picking grain on the Sabbath: "If you had understood the meaning of the words: 'What I want is mercy, not sacrifice,' you would not have condemned the blameless." Mt 12, 7. In answer to questions from a scribe, Jesus recited the two great commandments. "Then the scribe said to him, 'You are right, Teacher; you have truly said that "he is one, and besides him there is no other"; and "to love him with all the heart, and with all the understanding, and with all the strength," and "to love one's neighbor as oneself,"—*this is much more important than all whole burnt offerings and sacrifices.*' When Jesus saw that he answered wisely, he said to him, 'You are not far from the kingdom of God.'" Mk 12, 28-34. He drove out of the temple in Jerusalem those who were buying and selling sacrificial victims, cattle, sheep and doves, and the money-changers. Jn 2, 13-17; Mt 21, 12-13; Mk 11, 15-19; Lk 19, 45-46.

Prayer. Jesus repeatedly taught that his followers should pray to the Father, persistently and privately. "Ask, and it will be given to you; search, and you will find; knock, and the door will be opened for you." Mt 7, 7. "And if you have faith, everything you ask for in prayer you will receive." Mt 21, 22. "Anything you ask for from the Father he will grant in my name." Jn 16, 23.

Jesus shows his command of human psychology when he teaches the virtue of persistence in prayer. Even though, as he said, "Your Father knows what you need before you ask him," Mt 6, 8, he knew men and women would get discouraged with repeated praying. So he urges us to persist in prayer even to the point of being a pest about it, like the man who tried to borrow bread from his friend at midnight, Lk 11, 5-8, or the widow who kept pestering the unjust judge, Lk 18, 1-8.

The prayer Jesus called for is to be a private devotion, not a public and ritualistic activity: "When you pray, go to your private room and, when you have shut your door, pray to your Father who is in that secret place, and your Father who sees all that is done in secret will reward you." Mt 6, 6. There are no longer to be sacred places for worship. To the Samaritan woman at the well, Jesus said, "Believe me, woman, the hour is coming when you will worship the Father neither on this mountain nor in Jerusalem. . . . True worshipers will worship the Father in spirit and truth." Jn 4, 21, 23.

Reflections. Jesus prescribed and defined a new and different kind of religion, one without rules, rituals, prescribed observances and prohibitions, ostentatious public prayers or sacrifices. The world had never heard of such a religion. Jesus taught that worship, as well as the practice of the key virtues, was a matter of a change of mind and of habitual disposition, not a matter of external observances and practices. He taught a grown-up religion to people not ready to leave their immature rituals. When he counseled prayer in secret, he intended not rote prayers, but regular and frequent reflective analysis, self-examination and meditation, as the necessary means to make progress in developing and maintaining the key virtues of non-violence, non-judging, forgiveness, humility, and detachment from possessions in one's mind and heart. "When you are praying, do not heap up empty phrases as the Gentiles do; for they think that they will be heard because of their many words. Do not be like them, for your Father knows what you need before you ask him." Mt 6, 7-8.

What is the use of prayer if God already knows whether the prayer will be answered or not? Recall the discussion of the meaning of the eternal life of God in Chapter IV. God does not change. God's mind is not changed by prayer. God's mind never changes. God sees all at once the circumstances, the prayer, and the result. Thus it cannot be said that the prayer changed the result; but it also cannot be said that the result would have occurred if there had been no prayer. Prayer may or may not change events. It does change the person who prays. With regard to the efficacy of prayer, the only possible conclusion we can arrive at is that we can never be sure whether a given event is or is not an answer to prayer. We are left only with the repeated instruction from Jesus to pray persistently. I think that what Jesus intends is for each of us to experience the change which comes to the person who prays.

The discussion of the mission of Jesus in Chapter VI will shed more light on the reasons for the fierce anger Jesus showed in his opposition to the scribes and Pharisees. But one observation is pertinent here. Hans Küng argues that the Pharisees made light of sin:

"By their casuistry they [the Pharisees] isolate the individual sin. The requirement of obedience to God is split up into detailed, individual actions. Their primary concern is not with false basic attitudes, basic trends, basic dispositions, but with individual moral lapses, with drawing up lists of sins. These individual acts are registered and catalogued: . . . The dimension in depth of sin is never brought to light."[9]

This reminds me of the Church in which I was brought up. Some of you may have similar memories.

As part of his core teaching, Jesus was teaching a new definition of virtue and a new definition of sin. From this time forward, concentration should be focused on changing one's basic attitudes and dispositions, and not on observing detailed rules governing separate and specific acts. We are freed from detailed rules. This is what Jesus meant when he said that "You will know the truth, *and the truth will make you free.*" Jn 8, 51. This is what St. Paul meant when he said that "Now we are discharged from the law, dead to that which held us captive, so that we are slaves not under the old written code but in the new life of the Spirit." Rom 7, 6.

c.   **God, the Kingdom, and the Role of Jesus.**

Jesus's core teachings set forth a new context or framework for the key virtues and the new concept of religious practice. He gave us new teachings about God, announced the Kingdom of God, and taught about his own singular role in the new relationship between God and mankind.

God the Father. Because Judaism was a rigorously monotheistic religion, Jesus was able to assume that his listeners believed in a single all-powerful God, and he did not have to spend time teaching that doctrine. But Jesus made three significant and new additions to the Jewish idea of God. These new teachings provide a context or substructure within which we can understand how to practice the key virtues; much of what Jesus said about God appears in his teachings of the virtues of forgiveness and detachment from possessions.

First, Jesus taught that God is neither the vengeful, tribal God of the Old Testament nor a capricious, indifferent pagan god. Nor is God only the remote, abstract God of philosophers. God is, above all, a Father, with all the paternal virtues of a good human father, but in perfection. Before Jesus spoke, it was unknown to speak of God as a Father, but Jesus always did so, using an affectionate and intimate term, Abba, Father. God takes care of those who trust in him. Jesus said, "Therefore do not worry, saying 'What will we eat?' or 'What will we drink?' or 'What will we wear?' For . . . your heavenly Father knows that you need all these things. But strive first for the Kingdom of God and his righteousness, and all these things will be given to you as well." Mt 6, 31-32; Lk 12, 29-31. "Are not five sparrows sold for two pennies? Yet not one of them is forgotten in God's sight. But even the hairs of your head are all counted. Do not be afraid; you are of more value than many sparrows." Lk 12, 6-7. God forgives those who repent. "There will be more joy in heaven over one sinner who repents than over ninety-nine righteous persons who need no repentance." Lk 15, 7. Like the father of the Prodigal Son, God is always ready to forgive his children. Lk 15, 11-32.

Second, Jesus taught that God's justice and mercy are not always found in this life. The evil that befalls some people in life is not a punishment for sin. The good life that some other people enjoy is not a reward for virtuous conduct. Our Father "makes his sun rise on the evil and on the good, and sends his rain to fall on the honest and dishonest alike." Mt 5, 45. The farmer whose enemy sowed weeds in his wheat field does not let his field hands weed the fields, lest in gathering the weeds they would uproot the wheat. "Let both of them grow together until the harvest; and at harvest time I will tell the reapers, Collect the weeds first and bind them in bundles to be burned, but gather the wheat into my barn." Mt 13, 24-30, 36-43.

Jesus's disciples had a hard time understanding that misfortune is not a punishment for sin. When they saw a man who had been born blind, they asked Jesus, "'Rabbi, who sinned, this man or his parents, that he was born blind?' Jesus answered, 'Neither this man nor his parents sinned; he was born blind so that God's works might be revealed in him.'" Jn 9, 1-3. On another occasion, Jesus made the same point: "At that very time there were some present who told him about the Galileans whose blood Pilate had shed in the midst of their sacrifices. He asked them, 'Do you think that because those Galileans suffered in this way they were worse sinners than all other Galileans? No, I tell you; but unless you repent, you will all perish as they did." Lk 13, 1-3.

And finally, Jesus taught that God is love. "If anyone loves me he will keep my word, and my Father will love him, and we shall come to him and make our home with him." Jn 14, 23. "For God so loved the world that he gave his only begotten Son, that whosoever believes in him should not perish but have everlasting life." Jn 3, 16.

The Kingdom. Jesus's teachings about the Kingdom of Heaven, the community of those who accept his teaching and commit themselves to him, are more an announcement and a series of exhortations than a description. The Kingdom of Heaven is the community of men and women who have committed to the cultivation and practice of the key virtues. The Kingdom is also the new relationship of those men and women through Jesus to God, and to the fulfillment of God's plan for humanity. The particular structure of the Kingdom is not important. Jesus was wholly unspecific as to every practical detail of its organization. All men and women are called to the Kingdom, and there is a special emphasis on the call to sinners and outcast. "And indeed I did not come to call the virtuous but sinners." Mt 9, 13. God is insistent about the call to his Kingdom. In Jesus's parable of the great feast, the invited guests, one after another, made their excuses and did not come. The host became angry, and sent his servants out to the streets and lanes of the city, to bring in the poor, the crippled, the blind and the lame. When this did not fill the banquet hall, he said to his servant, "Go to the open roads and the hedgerows and force people to come in to make sure my house is full; because, I tell you, not one of those who were invited shall have a taste of my banquet." Lk 14, 16-24.

In his parables, Jesus foretold that the Kingdom would grow. "The Kingdom of Heaven is like a mustard seed that someone took and sowed in his field; it is the smallest of all the seeds, but when it has grown it is the greatest of shrubs and becomes a tree, so that the birds of the air come and make nests in its branches. . . . The Kingdom of Heaven is like yeast that a woman took and mixed in with three measures of flour until all of it was leavened." Mt 13, 31-33. As yeast changes the whole bread, the Kingdom will change the world. "You are the salt of the earth . . . . You are the light of the world." Mt 5, 13-14.

Entering the Kingdom of Heaven is difficult. "Try your best to enter by the narrow door, because, I tell you, many will try to enter and will not succeed." Lk 13, 24. "If anyone wants to be a follower of mine, let him renounce himself and take up his cross and follow me." Mk 8, 34; Mt 16, 24; Lk 14, 27. Entering the Kingdom is to be the highest priority and the overriding objective of those who believe in Jesus. "Strive first for the Kingdom of God." Mt 6, 33. "The Kingdom of Heaven is like treasure hidden in a field which someone has found; he hides it again, goes off happy, sells everything he owns and buys the field." Mt 13, 44. "For where your treasure is, there your heart will be also." Lk 12, 34. "No one who puts a hand to the plough and looks back is fit for the Kingdom of God." Lk 9, 62.

The Central Role of Jesus. Jesus taught that he himself had a unique and central role in God's Kingdom. The way to follow his teachings, he said, and the only way, is to follow his personal example as well as his teachings. We can become non-violent only if we follow his example of non-violence; we can become non-judging and forgiving only when we see and imitate him as non-judging and forgiving. We can imitate his humility and his detachment from possessions. In his life, we see that it can be done and that it has been done. "A disciple is no better than his master; he will be perfect if he is as his master is." Lk 6, 40. This is why we say not only that we believe him, but also that we believe in him.

The core teachings of Jesus are not simply revelations of propositions, but revelations of a person. In the Gospels, we hear Jesus revealing his personal belief system and his personal affective system, and we see him living a life conforming to those beliefs and affections. His core teachings are an extension of his personality, and of his unique perfection in knowledge and love of God. Over and over, he identifies himself with his message: "I am the bread of life . . . . Whoever eats of this bread will live forever." Jn 6, 48, 51. "I am the light of the world. Whoever follows me will never walk in darkness but will have the light of life." Jn 8, 12. "I am the resurrection and the life. Those who believe in me, even though they die, will live." Jn 11, 25.

Jesus claims that the identification of his message and his person is unique and perfect: "I am the way, and the truth, and the life. No one comes to the Father except through me." Jn 14, 6. "As a branch cannot bear fruit all by itself, but must remain part of the vine, neither can you unless you remain in me. I am the vine, you are the branches. Whoever remains in me, with me in him, bears fruit in plenty; for cut off from me you can do nothing." Jn 15, 4-5. "Come to me, all you who are weary and are carrying heavy burdens, and I will give you rest. Take my yoke upon you, and learn from me; for I am gentle and humble in heart, and you will find rest for your souls. For my yoke is easy and my burden is light." Mt 11, 28-30.

d. The Great Promises.

Jesus knew and frequently said that following his teachings would be difficult. To motivate people to follow him, Jesus made and frequently repeated three great promises. He promised:

1. That his followers will have eternal life;
2. That good people will be rewarded and evil people will be punished in the next life; and
3. That the Holy Spirit, or the Father, or the Son, will be with his followers forever.

Eternal Life. Jesus said:

> "There is no one who has left house, brothers, sisters, father, children or land for my sake and for the sake of the gospel who will not be repaid a hundred times over . . . now in this present time and, in the world to come, eternal life." Mk 10, 29-30; Mt 19, 29; Lk 18, 29-30.

> "For God so loved the world that he gave his only begotten Son, that whosoever believes in him should not perish, but have everlasting life." Jn 3, 16.

> "This is indeed the will of my Father, that all who see the Son and believe in him may have eternal life; and I will raise them up on the last day." Jn 6, 40.

"Very truly, I tell you, whoever keeps my word will never see death." Jn 8, 51.

"My sheep hear my voice. I know them, and they follow me. I give them eternal life, and they will never perish. No one will snatch them out of my hand." Jn 10, 27-28.

One of the most difficult of Jesus's teachings for people in our day to believe is that those who believe in him shall have eternal life. Yet this teaching of Jesus is repeated and clear. Further, he restored life to the dead at least three different times, and he himself rose from the dead and demonstrated his continued life after death to his apostles and disciples on many occasions.

Reward and Punishment After Death. There are many sayings of Jesus in which he speaks of the separation of the good from the evil in the last days. Here are some of them:

"The hour is coming when all who are in their graves will hear his [the Son's] voice and will come out—those who have done good, to the resurrection of life, and those who have done evil, to the resurrection of condemnation." Jn 5, 28-29.

"When then, just as the weeds are gathered up and burnt in the fire, so it will be at the end of time. The Son of Man will send his angels and they will gather out of his Kingdom all things that provoke offenses and all who do evil, and throw them into the blazing furnace, where there will be weeping and gnashing of teeth. Then the virtuous will shine like the sun in the Kingdom of their Father." Mt 13, 40-43.

"And if your eye should cause you to sin, tear it out; it is better for you to enter into the Kingdom of God with one eye, than to have two eyes and be thrown into hell where

their worm does not die nor their fire go out." Mk 9, 47-
48; Mt 5, 29-30; Mt 18, 8-9.

Jesus frequently said that "many are called, but few are
chosen," and several of his parables ended with people being "cast
into the outer darkness, where there is weeping and gnashing of
teeth." On the other hand, Jesus called himself the Good
Shepherd, who goes after every last sheep and brings him into
the fold. He said, "And this is the will of him who sent me, that
I should lose *nothing* of all that he has given me, but raise it up
on the last day." Jn 6, 39. Toward the end of his discourse at the
Last Supper, he prayed, "Father, the time has come; give glory
now to your Son, that your Son may give glory to you. You have
put him in authority over all mankind, to bring eternal life to *all*
those you have entrusted to him." Jn 17, 1-2.

I think Jesus meant us to live with a lifelong uncertainty
about whether we will be saved. We know that some will be
saved. We do not know that any will be damned. It is certainly
true that God's love for men and women is universal, and
that it is his desire and plan that all men and women come to
him through Jesus. I don't think we have sufficient reason to
conclude that this part of God's plan for humanity will be
frustrated.

God's Presence and Providence. Jesus many times promised
that God would be with his followers in this life, to provide
guidance and help when needed. Sometimes he called this the
presence of the Holy Spirit; other times he spoke of the continuing
presence of the Father, or of his own continuing presence. Here
is some of what he said:

> "When they take you before synagogues and magistrates
> and authorities, do not worry about how to defend
> yourselves or what to say, because when the time comes,
> the Holy Spirit will teach you what you must say." Lk 12,
> 11-12; Mt 10, 17-20; Mk 13, 11.

"And I will ask the Father, and he will give you another Advocate, to be with you forever. This is the Spirit of truth." Jn 14, 16-17.

"Those who love me will keep my word, and my Father will love them, and we will come to them and make our home with them." Jn 14, 23.

"But the Advocate, the Holy Spirit, whom the Father will send in my name, will teach you everything, and remind you of all I have said to you." Jn 14, 26.

"And know that I am with you always; yes, to the end of time." Mt 28, 20.

Jesus's promise of the Holy Spirit is, I think, a promise of something more than simply the general pervasive effect of God's providence toward men. He promised a special aid in times of special need to his followers, particularly in assuring that his own teachings would be remembered, properly understood, and eventually vindicated. As he said, the Holy Spirit "will teach you everything, and remind you of all I have said to you."

It seems to me that this promise must be understood in a framework of two significant limitations:

(a) The general principle of the economy of God is to be maintained. Humans have the ability and the duty to take advantage of the intelligibility of the universe to work out intelligent solutions to the problems of the world. This requires that there be regularity and predictability in the operation of natural forces, and so requires that divine power not intervene in a way which would materially interfere with the observable regularity and predictability of nature, or with the duty of men and women to work things out for themselves.

(b) Far too many Christians have claimed that they are justified in the course of morally repellent conduct because

God, or his Holy Spirit, has told them it is the right thing to do. In the name of Jesus, Christians have waged war, tortured prisoners, persecuted Jews and heretics, beaten women, and shot doctors who have performed abortions. The institutional Christian Churches, principally but by no means exclusively the Roman Catholic Church, have from time to time taught false doctrines and have laid insupportable burdens on their members in the name of the Holy Spirit.

Both of these limitations show the need for great care and considerable skepticism in discerning the action of the Holy Spirit. Jesus did not say he would send the Spirit to be a substitute for human judgment. When a person wonders whether he might be receiving a message from God, or from the Holy Spirit, careful reflection and study, good judgment, consultation with others where indicated, and common sense are required to separate the voice of the Spirit from the voice of one's own interests and passions.

The Completion of Jesus's Mission.

In John's Gospel, Jesus delivers an extended discourse after the Last Supper, the night before his death. Toward the end of that discourse, he prayed to his Father, and said, "I have glorified you on earth and *finished* the work that you gave me to do." Jn 17, 4. He had finished his teaching. This, his teaching, is what he meant by "the work that you gave me to do." His mission was accomplished. He had not yet died. No sacrifice in substitutionary atonement had yet taken place. But Jesus had finished his mission, and he said so. We are now in a position to determine why Jesus came, and what his mission was.

Notes:
1. McGrath, Alister E., *Christian Theology, An Introduction*, 3d ed. (Blackwell Publishers, 2001).
2. Armstrong, Karen, *A History of God* (Ballantine Books, 1994).
3. Kelly, Joseph F., *The Problem of Evil in the Western Tradition* (Liturgical Press, 2002).

4. Cahill, Thomas, *Desire of the Everlasting Hills* (Talese/Anchor Books, 2001), pp 91-92, 282.
5. Pascal, Blaise, *Pensées* (E.P. Dutton & Co., 1958), 150.
6. Quoted in Branch, Taylor, *Parting the Waters* (Touchstone, Simon & Schuster, 1988), p. 85.
7. Girard, René, *The Scapegoat* (Johns Hopkins University Press, 1977), p. 22.
8. Alison, James, *Raising Abel* (Crossroad Publishing Co., 1996), p. 35 (Emphasis added).
9. Küng, Hans, *On Being a Christian* (Image Books, Doubleday, 1976), p. 209.

VI

THE MISSION OF JESUS.

The Behaviors of Natural Selection.

We saw in Chapter II that humanity evolved from its animal ancestors with several genetically-imprinted behavior patterns which had evolved by natural selection: aggressive violence, kinship attachment and its associated suspicion, fear and hostility toward non-kin, dominant-submissive behavior, and acquisitiveness. These behavior patterns, unless strictly controlled, would make it difficult or impossible for large groups of humans to live together in peace. (The great apes, our nearest cousins in the animal world, generally live in very small kinship groups and do not seem to have ever succeeded in gathering a large tribe or clan together in peace.)

The development of the human brain and the human mind made this problem more difficult, not less so. For humans, imaginative powers make desire more general and less focused. We do not know what to desire. We have to learn it from others. So a human looks to see what another human desires, and when he or she sees what that is, that is what he or she wants. Put two toddlers in a room with a hundred toys. One will pick a toy to play with. The other will now desperately want that toy. None of the other toys will do. The development of the imagination and the need to learn what to desire from others makes violent conflict between humans more frequent and more passionate than among animals.

The Culture of Sacrifice.

In Chapter III, we explored humanity's earliest and most indispensable invention, the sacrifice. The primeval sacrifice released and satisfied the destructive force of violence within a community. The psychological transference of blame and guilt to the victim brought temporary peace to the community. The victim was made sacred and elevated to the status of a god. Girard observes that

> "The return to peace and order is ascribed to the same cause as the earlier troubles—to the victim himself. That is what makes the victim sacred and transforms the persecution into a point of religious and cultural departure."[1]

Humans developed rituals to enable them to reproduce the sacrificial transference when needed. The priests in charge of the sacrifice imposed prohibitions and taboos, the first moral codes, expressing them as the commands of the deity. Religious or cult solidarity was superimposed on kinship loyalty, and the community's instinctive suspicion and hostility toward strangers was reinforced within a controlled setting. Primitive sacrificial communities developed hierarchies, reinforcing the instinctive need for dominant-submissive relationships. With the social disciplines of a sacrificial community, the successful community could grow larger, and have greater success waging war against its neighbors. With this as its base, human culture was able to begin and grow. The complex of ritual acts and psychological transferences could be embodied in myths, prayers and sacred art. It is true to say that all human culture is rooted in the culture of sacrifice.

The most ancient civilizations showed all the elements of this prehistoric past. All were violent; the sacred king led an army of warriors, another specialized class or caste. Their myths and rituals were founded on violent acts, and violence, particularly reciprocal or imitative violence, an eye for an eye and a tooth for a tooth, was still permitted, even legislated. The unity of the people always depended on their sense of difference from, and their hatred or fear of, the neighboring nations or communities. They all had a class or caste system, with a concentration of wealth and status as well as power in the hands of the nobles (the kings, their families and the warriors) and the priests. Sacrifice, and its accompanying rituals, myths, cleanness and dietary rules, and taboos and prohibitions, were common to all. This is the culture of sacrifice, because all these elements are interwoven in a powerful cultural unity. This unity gave the culture of sacrifice a powerful survival and staying power; indeed, many of the characteristics of the nations of the culture of sacrifice persist in nations of our own day.

For all its strength and survival power, and in spite of the great accomplishments of many ancient civilizations, the culture of sacrifice is severely limited in its ability to foster, or even permit, the growth and development of mankind. Primal violence is its cultural base, and as long as that remains so, violence within the family, violence between members of the community, and violence between the community and other communities cannot be eradicated. All its myths and rituals are founded on the primal lie, the critical act of guilt-transference to the sacrificial victim, a scapegoat, and transferring blame or guilt to another is a primal urge of all men and women. As long as a person, a group or a nation remains locked in this self-deception, in which one looks for peace by transferring one's own guilt to another, or to another group of "different" people, peace among people and between nations can never be achieved. Look at the Israelis and the Palestinians. The hierarchies of priests and rulers which are required by the culture of sacrifice have locked societies into monarchies, theocracies, plutocracies and aristocracies, and in all of them, there has arisen a wide gulf between the rich and the poor, with social injustice and economic exploitation of the lower classes, the poor and the slaves. The myriad rules, regulations, prohibitions and taboos governing external conduct within the nations of the culture of sacrifice continue to impair the ability of each individual to develop his or her internally-directed and independent judgment and moral sense. The culture of sacrifice is a permanently immature cultural state, and, as long as it survives, it keeps men and women in an immature moral state as well.

The vices of the culture of sacrifice carry within them some relative virtues. Violence is close kin to the virtues of valor in battle and willingness to defend one's own people to the death. Transferring guilt and blame to the foreigner is closely related to the virtue of absolute loyalty to one's own community or people regardless of relative merit: "My country, right or wrong." Hierarchical organization makes governance of immature communities possible. Concentration of wealth and power, rules, rituals, observances and regular sacrificial ceremonies promote tribal and community unity. These relative virtues helped mankind emerge from prehistory to the glory that was Greece, the grandeur that was Rome, and the spiritual insights that were Israel. But by the time of Greece and Rome these tainted virtues had run their course; their limitations now exceeded their value.

The characteristics of every human childhood are docility, credulity, dependence, obedience and self-centeredness. These are virtues in the child but severe limitations in an adult. On maturation, these characteristics need to be replaced by skepticism, critical thinking, independence, self-direction, and concern and love for others. So in the childhood and adolescence of the human race, the survival and development of mankind depended on the childhood characteristics of the culture of sacrifice. For the maturation of mankind, these childhood virtues need to be replaced. But the culture of sacrifice has evolutionary stability. It is highly resistant to change, and it does not contain within it the principles to challenge itself. How could it be overcome and replaced? How could humanity progress toward its maturity?

The Teachings of Jesus.

The core teachings of Jesus, which we examined in Chapter V, comprise (a) a comprehensive criticism and condemnation of the culture of sacrifice, (b) a description of the culture of the Kingdom of Heaven, which Jesus intends to put in place of the culture of sacrifice, and (c) a call to all men and women to turn away from the culture of sacrifice and to the Kingdom of Heaven. Let us examine the extent and the depth of Jesus's criticism of the culture of sacrifice.

Violence and the Sacrifice. Jesus commanded absolute nonviolence. He expressly rejected "an eye for an eye and a tooth for a tooth." He required passive resistance to all evildoers. "If anyone strikes you on the right cheek, turn the other also." As we shall see, he did not desire or cooperate with his own execution, but he refused to offer violent resistance.

Jesus expressly condemned ritual sacrifice. He taught that his Father is a loving and merciful God who is not angry or wrathful and who does not desire sacrifice. He undermined the efficacy of sacrifice, its power to settle differences between disputants, when he said, "When you are offering your gift at the altar, if you remember that your brother or sister has something against you, leave your gift there before the altar and go; first be reconciled to your brother or sister, and then come and offer your gift." Mt 5, 23-24.

Kinship Loyalty and Hatred of the Enemy. Jesus expressly forbade judging or condemning another person, whether based on that person's conduct or upon his or her ethnic or religious group. "Let him who is without sin cast the first stone." Jn 8, 7. His frequently repeated rule, the rule of the Kingdom of Heaven, is that "the judgments you give are the judgments you will get." He even rejected kinship loyalty:

> "Then his mother and his brothers came; and standing outside, they sent to him and called him. A crowd was sitting around him; and they said to him, 'Your mother and your brothers and sisters are outside, asking for you.'

And he replied, 'Who are my mother and my brothers?' And looking at those who sat around him, he said, 'Here are my mother and my brothers! Whoever does the will of God is my brother and sister and mother.'" Mk 3, 31-35.

Jesus required his followers to forgive anyone who offends. He taught us to pray, "Forgive us our trespasses as we forgive those who trespass against us."

Hierarchy and Dominant-Submissive Behavior. Jesus preached a total inversion of hierarchical relationships. "I have come to call not the righteous but sinners." Mt 9, 12. "Whoever becomes humble like this child is the greatest in the Kingdom of heaven." Mt 18, 4. "The Son of Man came not to be served but to serve." Mt 20, 28. "So the last will be first, and the first will be last." Mt 20, 16. Jesus was particularly critical of members of the religious hierarchy. "Whenever you pray, do not be like the hypocrites, for they love to stand and pray in the synagogues and at the street corners, so that they may be seen by others. Truly I tell you, they have received their reward." Mt 6, 5. In defiance of Jewish proprieties, Jesus ate and drank with public sinners and outcasts, men and women alike. He told his disciples, "You are not to be called rabbi, for you have one teacher, and you are all students." Mt 23, 8. And he strongly criticized the scribes and Pharisees for their institutional hypocrisy.

Acquisitiveness and Wealth. Jesus repeatedly exhorted his disciples to trust that God would provide, as he provides for the birds of the air and the lilies of the field. He recommended strict poverty, and required at the least a detachment from possessions. The Kingdom of Heaven is for the poor in spirit. Mt 5, 3.

Rules, Rituals and Practices. Jesus rejected all the petty public observances and proscriptions of the culture of sacrifice. Holy times: he repeatedly went out of his way to break the rules of the Sabbath as then practiced. Holy places: "The hour is coming when you will worship the Father neither on this mountain nor in Jerusalem." Jn 4, 21. Ritual cleanness: "Oh, you Pharisees! You clean the outside of cup and plate, while inside yourselves you are filled with extortion and wickedness." Lk 11, 39. Dietary rules: "What goes into the mouth does not make a man unclean; it is what comes out of the mouth which makes him unclean." Mt 15, 11. In the Kingdom of heaven there is simply a change of mind, and persistent private prayer.

The Focus of the Teachings. There are a great many virtues, and many lists of virtues. Jesus could have taught any number of them. Did he? Take, for example, the list of so-called "cardinal" virtues: prudence, justice, fortitude and temperance. Are these important to human life? Of course. Did Jesus teach anything about any of them? No, he didn't. Take another list of virtues, from the Boy Scout promise: a scout is trustworthy, loyal, helpful, friendly, courteous, kind, obedient, cheerful, thrifty, brave, clean and reverent; a perfect list of the virtues a congregation hopes to find in its priest or minister. Did Jesus preach about any of these? No. Jesus selected five virtues, non-violence, non-judging, forgiveness, humility and detachment from possessions, and he preached them over and over. It is not a coincidence that each of these specific virtues directly opposes a specific anti-social naturally-selected behavior pattern we all have in our genes. It is not a coincidence that each of these specific virtues directly opposes a fundamental principle of the culture of sacrifice. Jesus's teachings reveal a plan and a program. His goal was to lead men and women to reject the culture of sacrifice and replace it with the Kingdom of Heaven. His method was to persuade each person to change his or her mind and heart, to reject in a very specific and direct way the behavior patterns of natural selection and of the culture of sacrifice, and to replace them with their direct opposites, the key virtues of the Kingdom of Heaven.

Did Jesus have in mind a "culture of sacrifice" to which he was opposed and against which he directed his teaching? I have described the culture of sacrifice (a) in terms of the behavior patterns of humans which evolved in our pre-human ancestors by natural selection, which presupposes the discoveries of Darwin and the twentieth-century evolutionary psychologists, and (b) in terms of the cultural and religious patterns of prehistoric and ancient cultures throughout the world, which presupposes the anthropological and ethnological discoveries of the last two centuries. Could Jesus have seen the cultures of mankind in this way?

Actually, he did, and he said so. What I have called the culture of sacrifice he called the world, the flesh or the devil. Jesus several times described himself as engaged in a struggle for the souls of mankind against a resistant, deceitful and implacable adversary:

> To his brothers: "The world cannot hate you, but it does hate me, because I give evidence that its ways are evil." Jn 7, 7.

> To his disciples: "It is the spirit that gives life; the flesh is useless. The words that I have spoken to you are spirit and life." Jn 6, 63.

> To the Jews: "You are from below, I am from above; you are of this world, I am not of this world." Jn 8, 23.

> To the Jews: "You are from your father the devil, and you choose to do your father's desires. He was a murderer from the beginning and does not stand in the truth, because there is no truth in him. When he lies, he speaks according to his own nature, for he is a liar and the father of lies. But because I tell the truth, you do not believe me." Jn 8, 44-45.

> To the crowd in Jerusalem: "Now is the judgment of the world; now the ruler of this world will be driven out. And I, when I am lifted up, will draw all men to myself." Jn 12, 31-32.

> To his disciples: "If the world hates you, be aware that it hated me before it hated you. If you belonged to the

world, the world would love you as its own. Because
you do not belong to the world, but I have chosen you
out of the world—therefore the world hates you." Jn
15, 18-19.

The "world" is not the sinners; Jesus came to call and save the
sinners. The "world," as Jesus used the term, is the culture of
sacrifice, which hates Jesus because he gives evidence, in his
teachings, that its ways are evil. The culture of sacrifice, personified
as the devil, is "a murderer from the beginning," because its central
act is the ritual sacrifice of an innocent victim. The culture of
sacrifice, personified as the devil, is "a liar, and the father of lies,"
because the critical psychological transference of guilt and blame
from the community to the sacrificial victim is a lie, the fundamental
and primal lie. Jesus opposed the culture of sacrifice with the
truth: "the words that I have spoken to you"; "I give evidence
that its ways are evil"; and with his life, "when I am lifted up."
Jesus declared victory over the culture of sacrifice: "Now is the
judgment of the world; now the ruler of this world will be driven
out." But he said the struggle would continue for his followers:
"Therefore the world hates you." We are still engaged in that
struggle.

Virtually every core teaching of Jesus strikes directly at a pillar
of the culture of sacrifice. This explains his anger, and the
vehemence of his attacks on the priests, the scribes and the
Pharisees, some of whom were undoubtedly good, well-meaning
souls who had just not gotten the message. Jesus was not attacking
individuals; he was attacking a massively corrupting system. He
was not attacking Judaism alone. Israel happened to be a classic
model of a nation of the culture of sacrifice, and the best and
most highly developed model. But Jesus was seeking to undermine
and transcend not just the culture of the Jewish nation, but the
underlying culture of all nations, of the whole world.

Jesus's core mission was to change the direction of mankind,
by announcing the death of the old order, the culture of sacrifice,
and the birth of the new order, the Kingdom of Heaven, based

on the new virtues of non-violence, non-judging, forgiveness, humility, detachment from possessions, and private prayer. This is why he came, and this is what he set out to do. This is how mankind is to be redeemed.

This is the second half of God's creation of humanity. The childhood and adolescence of humanity is over. Jesus taught the virtues and practices of the adulthood of humanity. He said that it would be difficult. He said that the changes he called for were required in the lives of all men and women. He said that the changes would ultimately prevail. He called the adulthood of humanity, of every man and woman, the Kingdom of Heaven. In the Kingdom, each one of us will be united with God through Jesus, and the world will be changed.

The Redemption of Humanity.

Let us return to the idea of redemption. As we saw in Chapter I, the redemption of humanity presupposes two things: (1) that in some way humanity needs to be redeemed or saved, and (2) that the human condition is such that the redeeming action will be effective to cause the redemption to occur. So the first question is whether humanity needed to be redeemed or saved from something, and if so, what?

What We Are To Be Redeemed From. There is a germ of truth in the myth of the Fall of Adam and Eve. While there was actually no sin of Adam and Eve, and no Fall from a state of original perfection, it is true that there are strong inclinations toward bad conduct in all humans without exception. These inclinations to do evil are firmly implanted in the human genome by natural selection. They consist of the genetically-based antisocial behaviors of violence, fear and hatred of strangers, dominant-submissive behaviors and acquisitiveness.

The culture of sacrifice began, grew and became universal because it did not resist these behavior patterns. Instead, early humans developed cultural institutions which channeled and controlled these behaviors in a way which allowed larger groups of humans to survive when bound together in a sacrificial community, first in tribes, then in ancient cities, and then in nations and empires. The culture of sacrifice cannot overcome violence, ethnic hatred, dominant-submissive patterns and acquisitiveness precisely because it was built on them and depends on them. As civilization has progressed, these behaviors have continued, while the ability of the culture of sacrifice to keep them under control has decreased with the decline of the controlling powers of myth, ritual and uniform religious observance.

Can humanity work its way out of the limitations of the culture of sacrifice without divine intervention? In several of the works on Darwinian behaviorism or evolutionary psychology which I read in the preparation of Chapter II, the authors recognized the persistence of the genetically-implanted behavioral tendencies of humans, particularly violence, and gave their respective recommendations for improving the human situation and controlling these behaviors. Michael Ghiglieri recommended calculated cooperation with others, stricter criminal law enforcement, and greater reliance on the principles of the *lex talionis* (an eye for an eye).[2] Irenaus Eibl-Eibesfeldt thought a strong world government would help.[3] Robert Wright praised the utilitarianism of Bentham and Mill (seek the greatest happiness for the greatest number) as a practical ground for moral conduct.[4] Ghiglieri and Wright both found considerable merit in Robert Axelrod's theory and method of cooperation, in which one is to act cooperatively toward another until and unless the other fails to cooperate, in which case one immediately retaliates in a measured and limited way.[5]

These are thoughtful suggestions, but I suggest that they are too intellectual and too calculated to serve as moral guides to ordinary humans. Controlled and limited retaliation for another's fault or failure is after all not a new idea; it is the *lex talionis*. The command of the Lord (in Ex 21, 24-25 and in Lev 24, 20) that retaliation for wrongdoing be "eye for eye, tooth for tooth, hand for hand, foot for foot, burn for burn, wound for wound, stripe for stripe" was meant to limit retaliation, not encourage it. But if history teaches us anything, it teaches that retaliation almost inevitably exceeds the original injury, and provokes a reciprocal and escalated response in return. Utilitarianism is an ethical philosophy which requires tranquil reflection, broad education and sophisticated moral judgment. Measured and carefully calibrated retaliation requires dispassionate control and restraint. Neither of these, it seems to me, can be relied upon to guide and control normal human emotional reactions and passions in a threatening or violent situation.

In times of stress, humans will almost invariably revert to their instinctive behaviors within the controlling structures of the culture of sacrifice. Take, for example, the response of the United States to the terrorist bombings of September 11, 2001. Whatever the merits of the country's response, it is true that there was immediate and almost unanimous support for violent retaliation against someone. There was immediate and unanimous demonizing of all "terrorists" and of the nations which "harbored" terrorists. There were public demonstrations of the kinship unity of the nation, particularly at sporting events. There was almost universal acceptance of the assumption of arbitrary powers by the executive branch of the government, including the waging of an undeclared war on Afghanistan, the detention for many months without charge and without counsel of thousands of men, most of whom shared nothing with the dead terrorists except a common ethnicity and religion, and repeated (mostly unsuccessful) attempts to stifle or suppress dissent or criticism of administration policy. This response is a perfect illustration of the continued power of the culture of sacrifice, and of its evolutionary stability and resistance to change. I conclude that history and current events both give substantial support to the conclusion that humans are incapable of changing the culture of sacrifice or growing out of its limitations without divine intervention.

How Redemption Will Be Effective. Given that Jesus called for the rejection of the culture of sacrifice and for its replacement with the Kingdom of Heaven, is there reason to hope and believe that his program will work? And if it does work, can the change so worked in humanity properly be called a redemption? We don't know the answers to these questions yet, because Jesus's program and mission have been so misunderstood and misconstrued over the last two thousand years. As G. K. Chesterton said, "The Christian ideal has not been tried and found wanting. It has been found difficult, and left untried."[6]

I believe that Jesus's program can work for the following reasons:

1.   Jesus's program sets forth a direct and complete method for overcoming the culture of sacrifice: the personal cultivation by many people, working together and supporting each other, of the habits of mind and the habits of conduct which are directly antithetical to the genetic behaviors of humans and the foundations of the culture of sacrifice: non-violence, non-judging, forgiveness, humility, detachment from possessions. If these virtues were to become habitual in a large portion of any society, that society would change in a fundamental way.

2.   The teachings of Jesus are clearly and forcefully expressed. They are understandable by all people whatever their level of education. The teachings speak to the whole person, involving the listener emotionally as well as intellectually.

3.   The incentives Jesus offers to those who follow his teachings mobilize one's highest and lowest motives. What is offered is personal happiness forever, the glory of God, the loving fraternity of other followers of Jesus, and the freeing of humanity from the bonds of the culture of sacrifice, from fear, hatred, oppression and want. The Great Promises have provided a powerful motivation and attraction to men and women for twenty centuries, and they will continue to do so.

4.   We have the personal example of Jesus, who called all of us to conform our minds and hearts to his, and who showed us by his life and death that the life of the Kingdom of Heaven can be lived.

5.   We have the example of many dedicated Christians

throughout the centuries who followed Jesus's teachings and accomplished much good for the people whose lives they touched.

6. And ultimately Jesus's call to the Kingdom is the only program out there which seems to speak to the fundamental problems and needs of humanity with a set of emotionally and rationally persuasive proposals for action and for change.

Because the behaviors to be overcome are in our genes as well as in our cultures, every single human being has to go through the process of ordering his own consciousness so that he or she achieves control over the instinctive behaviors of humans while keeping his or her intellectual and emotional balance. So Jesus's call to "change your mind" is a call to every single human being, and every person must participate in his or her own change. It is this change, and the changed person acting within the "new person" he or she has become, which I believe is the true redemption of every person, and thus the redemption of humanity.

Why This Way? Why in the world did God choose to redeem mankind this way? One person, two thousand years ago, preaching and teaching for three years; that's it? I suggest that the redemption of humanity, understood this way, is another example of the economy of God: God generally intends people to work things out for themselves. We must do much of the heavy lifting involved in our redemption ourselves. Jesus performed his part of the task: he taught his teachings and lived his life. It has been and remains the task of people like ourselves to hear his teachings, cultivate them, preserve them, act upon them, and pass them on to the next generation. It is the task of ordinary people like us to reflect on the teachings of Jesus, to decide how they are to be put into practice and incorporated into our lives, and to establish and administer such institutions and social structures as may be needed to accomplish the purpose of the teachings. As we shall see in Chapter VIII, the historical record so far is decidedly mixed.

The Fullness of Time.

With this view of the redemption of mankind, I think we can see, if dimly, why God proceeded with his plan for mankind in this way, and what St. Paul meant when he said, "*When the fullness of time had come*, God sent his Son, born of a woman, born under the law, in order to redeem those who were under the law." Gal 4, 4-5. The source and cause of humanity's redemption is the teaching and example of Jesus. Teaching like that of Jesus could only be heard, retained, recorded and spread through the world by natural human historical processes if it was delivered to the populace of an intellectually sophisticated and developed nation and people. That could be found in first-century Israel. Jesus began his preaching by announcing, "*The time is fulfilled,* and the Kingdom of God is at hand." Mk 1, 15. There was a right time for his redemptive activity.

Consider the following: First, we find another instance of the economy of God. Humans have the capacity to develop many sound and true religious and moral principles on their own, without special revelation from God. The humans of ancient times did so. Before Jesus came, humanity developed monotheism; basic moral rules, of which the ten commandments are one example; principles of justice, good faith, and magnanimity; and so forth. These developments were expressed and preserved in great works of literature, many of which were written between the eighth and the fourth centuries B.C.: the Old Testament, the Tao of Lao-Tsu, the Upanishads and the Bhagavadgita, the dialogues of Plato, and the teachings of Aristotle, among others. Jesus was able to concentrate his teaching activity on the rejection of the culture of sacrifice and its replacement with the Kingdom of Heaven. Humanity had already laid the groundwork. God had allowed humanity to progress as far as it could with its own abilities.

Second, Jesus's teachings needed to be presented in a time and place where the culture and the actual practice of sacrifice was still taken seriously (as it was not, for example, in Rome). Israel was such a place, but it ceased to be so after the Romans destroyed it in 70 A.D. Jesus's life and teaching had to occur at a time when the custom and practice of historical writing was widespread, so that his words and acts could be recorded with some accuracy and permanence. And it was helpful and perhaps essential for the survival and spread of Jesus's teachings that for the two or three centuries immediately following his death, the Mediterranean world was relatively peaceful and prosperous, and travel and communication over long distances was possible and practical.

Observe that if all that was needed for the redemption of humanity was that the Son of God must become man and offer himself as a sacrifice to God, that could have happened at any time. It could have taken place in 100,000 B.C. God would then have simply announced at some later time that it had taken place, as the Fall of Adam and Eve was announced to us long after it is said to have occurred. Only if the teaching itself and its spread by natural means were both critical elements of Jesus's redemptive activity is there a "fullness of time," a time when the teaching could and would be heard, remembered, recorded, and taught to others.

In keeping with the principle of economy, God chose one man, Jesus, born in about 4 B.C. in Israel. God expanded Jesus's natural human consciousness of God to the maximum point consistent with his still remaining a man, and did so from the moment of his conception throughout his life. By doing so, he entered into such a union with the man Jesus that it can be said that Jesus, while remaining a man, was truly God. That was the extent of this extraordinary intervention by God. Jesus lived unnoticed by history for thirty years, and then began a remarkable short public life of teaching and miracle-working for three years or so. During that short career, Jesus taught that the time had come for a revolutionary change, or, more accurately, a major evolutionary step, in the life of mankind. He assumed that men and women of good will would lead their lives according to the natural law, and concentrated his teachings on the need to develop the particular virtues which would (a) oppose and counteract the genetically-based behaviors of humans and the culture of sacrifice which was built on those behaviors and (b) replace them with a new and higher form of human civilization and culture. He taught that God is a loving Father to every man and woman, that the exclusive way to reach God is through him, and that those who followed him would receive the eternal life of union with him and with the Father.

I therefore conclude that the mission of Jesus was to teach all men and women the way to overcome the limitations and evils of our genetic inheritance and of the culture of sacrifice and to replace them with the culture of the Kingdom of Heaven. In the first half of creation, God created humanity with the capacity to progress from animal life to the high civilizations of the ancient world, by fierce and difficult channeling and control of humanity's genetically-imprinted anti-social behaviors. In the second half of creation, Jesus gave men and women in word and in personal example what we need to overcome those genetically-imprinted behaviors and the culture which was built on them, and thus to progress to a full human life in which humans will be peaceful, equal, unprejudiced, full of love for our fellow humans, and in control of our own lives. As each man and woman undertakes this task, he or she will develop the human strength and virtue which aligns us with God's will for each person. His or her capacity for God-consciousness will be able to expand, and he or she will grow toward union with Jesus and with God. This is what Jesus meant when he spoke of the Kingdom of Heaven. This is why God became man in Jesus.

A Summary of the Kingdom Explanation.

Let us call the explanation of the mission of Jesus here set forth the "Kingdom explanation," and compare it with Anselm's explanation. I believe that the Kingdom explanation is greatly preferable to Anselm's (the traditional Christian) explanation for the following reasons:

1. The Kingdom explanation is grounded in modern evolutionary biology, comparative anthropology and ethnology.

Anselm's explanation is grounded in the Genesis creation myth, particularly in one aspect of the myth, the original state of sinless perfection of humans, which is demonstrably false, and in obsolete feudal notions of honor and atonement.

2. The Kingdom explanation presents one divine plan for humanity, implemented in two parts, and provides reasons for the separation between the two parts. Anselm's explanation tells us that God's original plan for mankind was a failure, and that the life and death of Jesus was God's fallback position, his Plan B.

3. There is no place in the Kingdom explanation for the biological inheritance of sin, blame or guilt, while this concept, with its pernicious consequences, is essential to Anselm's explanation. The presence in the genes of all humans of inclinations toward anti-social behavior, placed there by natural selection, does not amount to human sin or guilt or human depravity. It's simply a biological fact. It separates us from God only in the sense that it impedes the development of God-consciousness in every one of us.

4. Anselm's explanation describes God as angry and wrathful, a God who demands the blood sacrifice of his only Son, and (in the person of the Son) as loving and caring at the same time. This is a schizophrenic God, or it is simply two different Gods. The Kingdom explanation describes God as a being who is steadfastly and consistently powerful and loving, but who consistently allows humans to make their own mistakes and learn from them; God treats humans as responsible adults.

5. In the Kingdom explanation, humans are fully involved in their own redemption. Jesus provided the teaching and the example. Every person must contend with his or her own genetic inheritance and against the limitations placed upon him or her by the culture of sacrifice. Every person who follows Jesus's teachings will help to build the Kingdom of Heaven in place of the culture of sacrifice, as so change and redeem the world. In Anselm's explanation, redemption is accomplished without the personal involvement of the redeemed person, who needs do nothing except receive and acknowledge the gift.

6. The Kingdom explanation makes Jesus's principal activity, his teaching, the redeeming action. Anselm's explanation ignores Jesus's teaching and his life, and gives exclusive importance to his passion and death, during which Jesus was essentially passive.

7. Anselm's explanation depends upon the wholly and deeply pagan notion that the proper way to please God is sacrifice, preferably human sacrifice. The Kingdom explanation treats human sacrifice as the source of the problem, not the solution, and as murder which cannot be defended or justified.

8. Anselm's explanation depends on the assertion that responsibility and guilt for sin can be transferred to another and assumed by another, so that the sinner is no longer responsible for the sin. This is the lie, the act of self-deception, the transference of guilt to the victim, which underlies the primeval sacrifice. In the Kingdom explanation, each man and woman is responsible for his and her own conduct, and remains so.

At this point, many readers will have concluded that Anselm's explanation is seriously flawed, and is almost certainly indefensible. But some readers may be unsure about some of the parts of the Kingdom explanation as I have set it forth. Let me clarify and summarize the argument, and identify some parts of the foregoing discussion which are not essential to acceptance of the Kingdom explanation.

There can be no doubt about the existence of the biologically derived and genetically-based behaviors of humans described in Chapter II. But some readers may be hesitant to accept Girard's theory of the origin of sacrificial religion and its central position in the development of human culture described in Chapter III. Girard's theory is based on his close analysis and explication of ancient myths, and in part on what was left out of those myths, and it has not been received entirely without controversy. My own view is that Girard's analysis is extraordinarily revealing, full of valuable insights, and basically true. But acceptance of his entire theory is not essential to the Kingdom explanation. What is necessary for the Kingdom explanation are only the observations that (i) virtually all ancient civilizations were violent hierarchical societies engaged in continual warfare against other nations and in violent subjugation of their own lower classes; (ii) sacrificial religions were at the heart of the cultures of these civilizations; and (iii) the culture of such civilizations and religions channeled and controlled, but did not oppose, the genetically-based antisocial behaviors which are in the genes of all humans. These observations are in their general outline unassailable.

Other readers may be unsure of the theory of the person of Jesus set forth in Chapter IV. I find that theory very helpful in trying to understand who Jesus was and what was his relationship to God. But what is necessary to the Kingdom explanation are only the conclusions that (i) Jesus was fully and truly a human being; and (ii) Jesus had a special and wholly unique relationship with God and a special and wholly unique mission to the rest of humanity.

Finally, readers who are unsure about the analysis and organization of Jesus's teachings which I have set forth in Chapter V are welcome to take out their own copy of the Gospels and construct their own analysis and organization of Jesus's teachings. I have some confidence that they will come to substantially the same conclusions as I have.

So the argument for the truth of the Kingdom explanation in summary form is as follows:

1. All humans have in their genes certain naturally-selected behavioral tendencies toward violence, judging and transferring blame to others, dominant-submissive relationships, and acquisitiveness.

2. Nearly all human societies have channeled and controlled these otherwise destructive genetically-based behavior patterns by incorporating them into their institutional structures and cultures. In ancient societies, sacrificial religions, rituals, rules and myths were important to the incorporation of these behaviors into human cultures. Such societies and their cultural institutions are evolutionarily stable; they are very difficult to change in any fundamental way; and their fundamental

characteristics severely limit the development and betterment of all human beings.

3. Jesus was a man with a unique relationship with God and a unique mission to mankind, which he carried out by teaching and working miracles for a few years in first-century Israel. An analysis of his teachings shows that his great theme or program was a comprehensive repudiation of the prevailing culture of human societies, here described as the culture of sacrifice, and a description of the Kingdom of Heaven which is to replace and transcend that culture. Much of his teaching called upon men and women to adopt and practice precisely those virtues which are specifically and directly opposed to the genetically-based antisocial behaviors of humanity. Jesus taught that if men and women followed his teachings and his personal example, they would receive eternal life and the world would be changed into a much better place. This is why Jesus came and what he came to do.

I have concluded, and I hope that the reader will have concluded, that the Kingdom explanation of the mission of Jesus is thoroughly defensible, and in its general outlines true and correct; and that the traditional Christian explanation of the mission of Jesus is not.

The Mission of Meaning and Hope.

An explanation of the mission of Jesus needs to be cogent, and consistent with scripture; but it needs more. The explanation must provide meaning and hope to the people who are called by Jesus to the difficult task of following him. Let us explore whether the Kingdom explanation offers meaning and hope to people of our day.

Douglas John Hall, following Paul Tillich, asserts that the dominant characteristic of the predicament of humanity in the modern age is "the anxiety of meaninglessness and despair."[7] I think this is true. But thoughts and feelings of meaninglessness and despair are so deeply rooted in our thought and so personal in our feelings that they are almost inarticulate in most of us most of the time. Part of the reason for this is that thoughts and feelings of meaninglessness and despair, when we dwell on them, incapacitate us from the task of living our ordinary lives. So we put them in the back of our minds and get on with daily living. The clearest way to approach these anxieties as feelings and thoughts we share, it seems to me, is for me to describe what the anxiety of meaninglessness and despair has meant to me in my own life, in the hope that some of my thoughts and experiences will resonate with those of the reader.

In earlier times, the meaning of life was that held and taught by the dominant cultural institutions, principally churches and church-related schools. That is no longer the case. We now live in a scientific, industrial and technological age, and in a society which both allows and demands great tolerance for one another's philosophical or religious beliefs. Within this age and society, each of us must individually find, or choose, a meaning for one's own life. Science and technology do not offer any guidance as to the meaning or purpose of human life, nor do scientists or engineers think it is within the scope of their calling to do so. Tolerance for the views of others as to the meaning and purpose of life is not the same as the view that all conclusions are of equal merit, but the one is close enough to the other that it is difficult to keep them separate in practice, and we all must consider whether it is possible that one set of philosophical or religious views can really be found or held to be superior to all other sets.

I did not begin my exploration of the Christian religion and of the mission of Jesus which led to this writing because of a desire to engage in theological speculation as an interesting field of study. I began and continued because I had sought a coherent and hopeful explanation of the meaning of life in traditional Christianity, and I did not find it there. I found instead a profound disconnect between the teachings of the Christian Churches and the culture of the modern world, my world. Traditional Christianity, both Protestant and Catholic, seemed in my limited experience to be explaining its central teachings in terms of mythology (the Fall of Adam and Eve), blood sacrifice (a pagan practice which is wholly foreign to modern man), arrangements concerning the fate of humanity negotiated between persons of the Godhead, in which humans did not meaningfully participate, and an invisible "supernatural" level of life in which "grace" flows here and there in mysterious and imperceptible ways. None of this seemed helpful or even relevant to my search for a meaning to modern life, nor to my own life as a person living in the twentieth and twenty-first centuries. And it has been my experience that the moral message of the traditional Christian Churches sets a standard no different from or higher than that of the secular society in which we live. So, like many other Christians, I suspect, I found no answer to the meaning of life in the Christian Churches, and I made do with a provisional ethic of conformity to the good secular standards of our society. This is my experience of the anxiety of meaninglessness.

The great despair of our age is our realization that our scientific and technological brilliance has multiplied the power of violence and of inter-ethnic and inter-religious hatred, and we don't know what to do about it. We saw, in the Second World War, that the most enlightened, cultured, sophisticated, and scientifically and technologically advanced nation in Europe could descend to barbaric murderous war against its neighbors and to the planned extermination of an entire people in the Holocaust. Intractable inter-ethnic and inter-religious hatred and violence continues to our day. We seem to have no idea how to respond except to arbitrarily choose a suitable target (yesterday Serbia, today Iraq, tomorrow Syria? Iran? Pakistan?) from among the many which we judge to be badly ruled, and to drop high explosive on the (generally innocent) people of the chosen target nation. The response of the Christian Churches to this, if any, has been muted and uncertain. The anxiety of despair seems to be the rational human response to our situation.

What we see in our world is the culture of sacrifice in

disintegration. The myths and creeds by which nations used to control the violence of their peoples have lost their force. They are no longer believed by modern men and women, and they cannot be resuscitated. They can no longer supply meaning, and they cannot stave off our despair. This is what I think is meant by the dominant characteristic of our modern age, the anxiety of meaninglessness and despair.

I suggest, and I personally believe, that in the Kingdom explanation of the mission of Jesus we can find meaning for our lives and hope for a better age. In the light of Darwinian anthropology or evolutionary psychology we see the actual condition of humanity and the roots of its most difficult problems. In the light of cultural anthropology, we see how the evolved behaviors of humans have been built into the fabric of the great civilizations and the great nations, ancient and modern. It is not a pretty picture, but it is a realistic picture of the world as we find it. One could despair of God for creating humanity in such a mess.

But God was not done creating humanity. The second half of creation, the life, teachings, death and resurrection of Jesus, completed God's creation by giving humanity the cure for the problem and a hope for the future. Jesus's message and program, as I have worked it out, calls all of us to resist and transcend the culture of sacrifice by cultivating the virtues and the habits of mind which will replace the culture of sacrifice with the Kingdom of Heaven here on earth. The meaning of human life is then that each one of us starts with disorders, in a society built on those disorders, and each by his or her own effort struggles to change the disorders within us into the order that is set forth in the life and teachings of Jesus. This realistic view of the meaning of life answers the anxiety of meaninglessness we have all felt. It also answers our feelings of despair by giving us hope that Jesus's program can and will work. We cultivate his key virtues, and we follow his example. We participate, by identifying with Jesus, in our own redemptions, person by person. We each make our personal garden grow. We do so by careful thinking, reflection, hard work, courage and persistence; our natural powers doing natural work on our own habits and ways of looking at the world. And, as we believe Jesus, we believe that our own efforts, and those of others doing the same, will change the world into a world of non-violence, non-judging, forgiveness, humility and detachment from possessions. This is the world we want for our children and grandchildren.

The key to the key virtues, as I said above, is non-judging. The followers of Jesus do not judge those who do not follow him. We do not exclude, or expel, because exclusion and expulsion are the way of the culture of sacrifice. All who work for a non-violent, non-judging, non-hierarchical, caring and forgiving world are welcome. Those who choose to follow Jesus are to be yeast, or salt, or the light of the world, and will not withhold yeast or salt or light from anyone. For those who see Jesus as teacher and as exemplar, there is meaning and hope in his mission, which becomes our mission. All who work for the same goals, whatever their beliefs, are our brothers and sisters in this mission. We have simply to live and work in the world as we know it, with the meaning and hope that Jesus's life and teachings provide, and let the yeast, the salt and the light do its own work.

Notes:
1. Girard, René, *The Scapegoat* (Johns Hopkins University Press, 1986), p. 55.
2. Ghiglieri, Michael P., *The Dark Side of Man* (Perseus Books, 1999), p. 256.
3. Eibl-Eibesfeldt, Irenaus, *The Biology of Peace and War* (Viking Press, 1979), pp. 233-35.
4. Wright, Robert, *The Moral Animal* (Vintage Books, 1994), pp. 330-42.
5. Axelrod, Robert, *The Evolution of Cooperation* (Basic Books, 1984).

6. Chesterton, Gilbert Keith, *What's Wrong with the World* (Dodd, Mead & Co., 1910), p. 37.
7. Hall, Douglas John, *Professing the Faith* (Fortress Press, 1993), p. 479.

VII

THE DEATH AND RESURRECTION OF JESUS.

The Confrontation.

As we have seen, in Jesus's time, Judaism was a sacrificial religion and Israel was a theocratic state. One component of its classic sacrificial religion was its innumerable prohibitions and rules of conduct, regulating external actions in minute detail, with complex dietary proscriptions, rules of ritual cleanness, rules for what could and could not be done on the Sabbath, and so forth. Another was that the priests not only promulgated and interpreted all the rules, but they intermediated between God and man. They alone could officiate at the sacrifice. Through their control of the rules, the prohibitions, the rituals and the sacrifices, the priests, the scribes and the Pharisees governed Israel, subject to the Roman presence, which was indifferent to their religion as long as public order could be preserved.

Jesus was a realistic man. He knew that his core teachings directly challenged the traditional rules and ritual practices of Judaism. He had expressly taught that the Sabbath rules were subordinate not only to acts of goodness, such as healing the blind and the lame, but also to the convenience of his disciples, as when they picked grain on the Sabbath. Jesus had gone out of his way to challenge the external rules of Judaism. The man born blind had been blind since birth, and there was no reason why Jesus could not have waited until Sunday or Monday to restore his sight. The woman in the synagogue had been crippled for eighteen years. The man at the sheepgate pool had been an invalid for thirty-eight years. He had cured them all on the Sabbath.

Jesus repeatedly forgave sins, usurping a role which Judaism reserved to its priests. He flouted the rules of ritual cleanness, and used each such ccasion to criticize the Pharisees for their hypocrisy and wickedness. Lk 11, 37-41. His teaching reversed the dietary rules: "What goes into the mouth does not make a man unclean; it is what comes out of the mouth which makes him unclean." Mt 15, 11. He attacked the very idea of sacrifice. "Go and learn the meaning of the words: 'What I want is mercy, not sacrifice.'" Mt 9, 13. And he condemned the scribes and the Pharisees in the strongest language. Mt 23; Lk 11.

Jesus knew what the consequences would be. He had attacked every element of the religious practice of Judaism, in the face of the leaders who depended on those elements for their authority, their power, their social position and their very self-esteem. He had gathered a large band of followers. He knew that the priests, scribes and Pharisees would use their power to silence him permanently. He knew that if he continued to preach the truth, and continued his commitment to non-violence, there was nothing he could do about it. He knew, and repeatedly told his disciples, that he would be put to death in Jerusalem. Mt 17, 23; 20, 17-19; Mk 9, 30-32; 10, 32-34; Lk 18, 31-34.

We have known in the last century two great self-sacrificing heroes (or saints) of non-violence, Mohandas Gandhi and Martin Luther King. From their lives and from their examples we have seen the strange and uncanny power of non-violence. We have also seen the practical consequences of continuing in non-violence to the end; in the cases of Gandhi and King, repeated imprisonment, and death by assassination; in the case of Jesus, torture and death in a sham legal process. Jesus knew that the example of his life would be completed and perfected only if he maintained his steadfast courage and his commitment to his mission with persistence through torture and death. He knew that the inevitable result of his commitment, his death on the cross, would become a powerful symbol for the spread of the Kingdom of Heaven. As he said, "When I am lifted up from the earth, I shall draw all men to myself." Jn 12, 32.

Why Was Jesus's Death Necessary?

Why exactly did the leaders of the Jews conspire to have Jesus killed? The traditional response of Christians, without giving it much thought, is that they were evil men; they were hypocrites, as Jesus said. Other explanations have been suggested. The chief priests and Pharisees had said to each other, "If we let him go on like this, everyone will believe in him, and the Romans will come and destroy both our holy place and our nation." Jn 11, 48. Some skeptical students of Christianity have suggested, based on this passage, that the leaders of the Jews feared that Jesus would lead an armed revolt against the Romans (as later Jewish zealots did) and that the Jewish nation would be crushed. But the suggestion that Jesus could or would lead an armed revolution is impossible to reconcile with the body of his teaching and works, just as the suggestion that he was a victim of a small band of evil men does not give them credit for understanding what was at stake. Let us rather assume that the chief priests, scribes and Pharisees of Israel were responsible members of the ruling class. If so, they would (and did) understand that the teachings of Jesus were subversive of the very foundation of the Jewish nation.

The nation of Israel was a classic nation of the culture of sacrifice. What made it such a nation was the common religious culture of the Jews, based on sacrifice; its national self-identity, which means that its people strongly felt that they were different from and better than their neighbors (witness their attitude towards the Samaritans); and the hierarchical structure of its society, rigidly bound together by the required observance of its myriad rules of religious practice. Since the borders of the nation of Israel were not clearly geographically defined, maintaining the sense of separation from and superiority to neighboring states was all the more important; judging (and feeling superior to) the neighboring states was all the more important; judging their neighbors, and hating them as enemies, was important.

The responsible political leaders of Israel had listened carefully to the core teachings of Jesus. They could only conclude that if the people really ever decided to follow those core teachings, all this could be swept away. There would be no more sacrifice; no more rules of diet, of cleanness, of the Sabbath; no more invidious separation from their non-Jewish neighbors; and no more priestly hierarchy. As far as they could see, Jesus's teachings, if really followed, would dissolve the Jewish nation. So he had to be gotten out of the way. As Caiaphas perceptively observed, "You know nothing at all! You do not understand that it is better for you to have one man die for the people, than to have the whole nation destroyed." Jn 11, 50.

Observe that, in the light of this analysis, the leaders of the Jews did *not* decide to have Jesus killed because they were good Jews, or even because they were bad Jews. They decided to execute Jesus because they were good pagans, for the culture of sacrifice which they were defending is pagan to its roots. If "the Jews" represented anyone, they represented the pagans, the heathens, of the culture of sacrifice. This is to say they represented all mankind, for almost all of us, including most Christians, are still to this day very much pagan. The apostles understood this. They expressed it this way shortly after Pentecost, in a prayer to God: "This is what has come true: in this very city Herod and Pontius Pilate *made an alliance with the pagan nations and the peoples of Israel,* against your holy servant Jesus whom you anointed." Acts 4, 27.

So the leaders of the Jewish nation, in alliance with the Romans, put together a plan to have Jesus executed, and they carried it out. They bribed one of the disciples, Judas, to tell them when Jesus would be alone or with just a few followers. They arrested Jesus at night, held a mock trial, sent him to Herod's court, got him back from Herod and brought him to Pilate early the next morning. The supporters of Jesus, and all his disciples, fled. The Jewish leaders assembled a mob to pressure Pilate, and by mid-morning, Pilate had had Jesus scourged, and had ordered that he be crucified. Jesus remained true to his teaching of non-violence, and since only violence could have saved him, he was not saved. He remained true to his teaching of not judging or placing blame, and from the cross he prayed that his murderers be forgiven. By mid-afternoon, he was dead. The Roman soldiers who had crucified him made sure of that. And by nightfall, he was buried in a tomb nearby.

The Resurrection.

On the third day Jesus rose from the dead. The first fact in the history of Christianity is the testimony and preaching of a considerable number of people, all of whom said that they had personally seen the risen Jesus. All of the remaining eleven apostles had seen the risen Jesus. When, after Jesus's ascension, they decided to select a twelfth apostle, to fill the place of Judas, their criterion was to choose a man who had followed Jesus for his entire public ministry and who had seen the risen Jesus. Acts 1, 21-22. All of the sermons recorded in the Acts of the Apostles have Christ's resurrection as their central theme. The resurrection was critical to St. Paul, who said, "If Christ has not been raised, then our proclamation has been in vain and your faith has been in vain." 1 Cor 15, 14. Belief in the resurrection preceded belief in the Gospels, because if the resurrection had not been believed there would have been no need for or occasion for the Gospels. No one would have bothered to write them.

The New Testament contains no fewer than nineteen references to appearances of the risen Jesus, describing about ten separate appearances, six of which are reported by two or three authors. Jesus appeared

1. to Mary Magdalene (Mk 16, 9; Jn 20, 14-17);
2. to Mary Magdalene and the other Mary (Mt 28, 9-10);
3. to two disciples on the road to Emmaus (Mk 16, 12; Lk 24, 13-32);
4. separately to Peter (Lk 24, 34; 1 Cor 15, 5) and James (1 Cor 15, 7);

5. to all the disciples except Thomas, the evening of the first day (Lk 24, 36; Jn 20, 19-23; 1 Cor 15, 5);

6. to all the disciples, a week later (Mk 16, 14; Jn 20, 26-29);

7. by the sea of Tiberias, to seven disciples (Jn 21, 1-23);

8. to all the disciples on a mountain in Galilee (Mt 28, 16-18);

9. to more than five hundred of the brethren, most of whom were still alive twenty-five years later, when St. Paul wrote of it (1 Cor 15, 6); and

10. at his ascension, to a large group of disciples (Mk 16, 19; Lk 24, 50-51; Acts 1, 6-11).

It is a substantial body of testimonial evidence. It is not plausible to believe that such a large group of people could have invented the story of the resurrection, formed a conspiracy to spread it, and then maintained that conspiracy for the rest of their lives. Some authors have suggested that the witnesses to the risen Christ were hallucinating, in the emotional grip of a wish to see Jesus again. But if they were hallucinating, why did they hallucinate someone they didn't recognize? Mary Magdalene saw Jesus, and at first thought he was the gardener. Jn 20, 15. The disciples on the road to Emmaus thought Jesus was a fellow traveler, and did not recognize him until after a long walk and a long conversation. Lk 24, 16. And none of the seven disciples who saw Jesus from the boat on the sea of Tiberias knew who he was. Jn 21, 4. These were not credulous or hysterical men and women. I assume that the average truck driver is more hard-headed than I. I think a Galilean fisherman is as hard-headed as your average truck driver. And Mary Magdalene was not inexperienced about men.

The way Jesus appeared is interesting. He did not appear as a vision, as a spirit, or as a ghost; he appeared as a man in the flesh. He bore the wounds of his death. It was not as if he had never been dead; he appeared as one who had been dead and was now fully alive. He could be touched. He could be, and was, mistaken for a gardener, or a fellow traveler on the road. On two occasions he joined his disciples in a meal of broiled fish. He was ordinary in these respects, except that he seemed to have gained a facility of appearing and disappearing. When the disciples fishing on the Lake of Tiberias saw him from the boat, and after some time recognized him, they came to the shore. There they found that the risen Jesus had built a charcoal fire and was grilling fish. "Come and have breakfast," he said. In a strange way, these words strike me as among the most encouraging and comforting things Jesus ever said. In contrast to the narratives of the incarnation, birth and early childhood of Jesus, the narratives of his appearances after his resurrection are not mythic or poetic, but appear to be direct testimony, simply documented.

The resurrection of Jesus is the single most important miracle of the life of Jesus. There are some learned and committed Christians who have difficulty believing this miracle, and many of us have difficulty some of the time believing that it actually took place. For example, the great theologian Hans Küng has written an extended and at times brilliant defense of belief in Jesus, *On Being a Christian*.[1] But Küng states that in his view the raising of Jesus from the dead was "contrary to the laws of nature,"[2] and that his appearances to his disciples "are contrary to both scientific thinking and the convictions and experiences of ordinary people," and "cannot be regarded as miracles canceling the laws of nature."[3] Küng admits that the apostles and disciples did in some way experience the living Jesus after his death, and that this experience radically and permanently transformed their understanding, their courage, and their subsequent conduct. He resorts to the most vague and obscure language to describe what this experience was, and what happened to the disciples, and to try to explain why they all described their experiences the same way, as the real appearance of the risen Jesus to them. As he explains it, "The corporality of the resurrection does not require the tomb to be empty. God raises the person in a new, different, unimaginable 'spiritual corporality.' As explained, the decisive thing is the new, eternal life in that ultimate, hidden reality which we call God."[4] What can this mean?

Küng clings to two questionable *a priori* assumptions, which he believes to be good science: (a) that God so ordained the laws of the natural universe that he retained no power to vary them for any reason, and (b) that those laws preclude the possibility of the resurrection of the dead. I explained in Chapter IV, in the discussion of the miracles of Jesus, why these views are no longer good science. Science and the experience of mankind certainly show that the resurrection of a person from the dead is (as far as we know) exceedingly rare and thus highly unlikely, but they cannot show that it is impossible. Whether we admit that it took place on one occasion depends on the evidence. I am a practicing lawyer, and in the law the best evidence is the testimony of an eyewitness. Other evidence is circumstantial, and it is frequently regarded as less reliable, as when we say, "Oh, the evidence against him was purely circumstantial" or "He was convicted on circumstantial evidence." The evidence described above, assuredly testimonial, strongly indicates that in this one case, an exception occurred: the dead Jesus did rise.

Improbable though this is, all the alternative explanations of the data are even more improbable. Clearly something quite extraordinary happened to the large group of men and women who had gathered around Jesus, shortly following his death. Clearly they described it as seeing the risen Jesus. If this did not happen, that is, if they didn't see the risen Jesus, then we must conclude that some other event or events, which no one has ever described, occurred, and that the other event or events caused a radical change in the understanding, courage and conduct of all these men and women. So we will have replaced a describable single miracle with fifty or five hundred indescribable miracles. We will then have to explain why, and how, this large group would have concocted a uniform and deceptive story of appearances of the risen Jesus, and would have maintained that conspiracy of deception to their deaths.

James Alison describes the commonly held modern view of the resurrection of Jesus as follows:

"The second starting point [for modern skepticism] is that the disciples *thought* that the resurrection was something objective that really happened to Jesus, and so described it the way they did. However, from the vantage point of 'modernity' or some such position of supposed superiority, we know better than they, and in the light of our more sophisticated philosophical techniques we are able to reread the texts and see that *in fact* what is being described is a subjective experience. . . . It is quite clear that whatever the apostolic witnesses are describing, it was something which broke the categories of easily available speech, something entirely new and unexpected, and furthermore something which they saw as definitive and unsurpassable. For us to claim that we understand it better than they is effectively to claim that it was not definitive and unsurpassable, because we, in our understanding, have surpassed it and are able to understand it. . . . It is as though that can only be accepted which can be digested within our frame of reference; that whose acceptance alters our frame of reference cannot be accepted."[5]

The resurrection of Jesus does alter our frame of reference. It was intended to do so.

I am skeptical about miracles, but I do not have an *a priori* conviction that they cannot occur. On the basis of the historical evidence, and the extreme implausibility of any other explanation, I conclude that God raised Jesus from the dead, and that Jesus appeared numerous times to his disciples. I arrive at this conclusion not by making an act or leap of faith, but as a reasoned conclusion based on the circumstances, on the evidence and on my life experience.

The resurrection of the crucified Jesus was not the mission of Jesus. His mission was to teach that all men must resist and transcend the culture of sacrifice by changing our minds and building the Kingdom of Heaven. His resurrection was a demonstration for the benefit of his disciples and all who would subsequently follow him of the truth, the authority and the power of his teaching.

The first thing that the appearance of the risen Jesus demonstrated is that God confirmed his life and teachings. God confirmed that Jesus had spoken truly of his unique relationship with and identity with God, confirmed the truth and significance of Jesus's teachings, particularly his core teachings, confirmed Jesus's crucial mediating role in the salvation of men and women and of the world, and confirmed Jesus's promises to all humanity.

Second, the resurrection showed that the primal lie, which is the psychological transfer of blame and guilt to the victim, whether the victim of a blood sacrifice, or a scapegoat, or a victim of persecution, is wholly wrong. By his death, Jesus actually accomplished the elimination of ritual sacrifice from the world. Ritual sacrifice has died out in every part of the world reached by the Christian message, even where few of the hearers became Christian. Ritual sacrifice "works" only because there is a real psychological transference of the blame and guilt of the community from the members of the community to the victim, the scapegoat, such that the victim is perceived to be truly guilty. The central Christian symbol of Jesus crucified on the cross and risen from the dead as a wholly innocent victim has made it impossible in any community touched by Christianity to believe any longer in the real guilt of any sacrificial victim. Once that happens, the required psychological transference cannot be made. Violence is still with us, but ritual sacrifices are not. James Alison puts it this way:

> "Jesus's resurrection did not only reveal that this man was, in fact, innocent; it did not only reveal that Jesus was right about God. It did much more: it revealed the whole mechanism by which innocent victims are created by people who think that by creating such victims they are working God's most holy will. That is to say, it left wide open the murderous and mendacious nature of all human religion, even in its best and purest form, the one practiced

by those who are, in truth, the chosen people of God, the
bearers of God's revelation.[6]

Third, the resurrection of Jesus showed that death is a passage,
not an end, for humans. The ancient language of the Preface
from the Christian Requiem Mass says it this way: "*Tuis enim
fidelibus, Domine, vita mutatur, non tollitur.*" "To your faithful,
Lord, life is changed, not ended." Jesus, a human like us, had
passed through death to life. By his resurrection, God confirmed
the teachings of Jesus, and Jesus had repeatedly taught that all
those who follow him will have eternal life. Because this is a
difficult teaching for men and women to believe, Jesus showed
us that it was true by showing us that a human person could and
did pass through death to life.

When the risen Jesus had completed his instructions to his
disciples over a period of time, probably about forty days, he
appeared at a gathering with a large group of disciples. He bade
them farewell, they saw him lift up into the air, and he disappeared
into a cloud.

Notes:
1. Küng, Hans, *On Being a Christian* (Doubleday Image Books,
   1976).
2. *Ibid.*, p. 359.
3. *Ibid.*, p. 375.
4. *Ibid.*, p. 366.
5. Alison, James, *The Joy of Being Wrong* (Crossroad Publishing
   Co., 1998), p. 72.
6. Alison, James, *Raising Abel* (Crossroad Publishing Co., 1996),
   p. 27.

VIII

THE FAILURE OF THE CHRISTIAN CHURCHES.

After Jesus had left them, the disciples returned to Jerusalem, where they stayed together. On the Jewish feast of Pentecost, they were "filled with the Holy Spirit" and went out to preach to the crowds which had gathered there. They preached, they baptized, and they added members to the community of the Lord; and these activities have continued to this day.

The disciples of Jesus had founded a new religion, the Christian Church. As far as we know, Jesus had never taught them anything about how to organize and structure a church, apart from his instructions to itinerant preachers (Mt 10, 1-41; Mk 6, 7-13; Lk 9, 1-6), which were not much help. Greater problems were created by the fact that what Jesus had taught in his core teachings and had revealed in his life, death and resurrection was too new and different to be grasped with any kind of clarity in the time of the earliest Christian Church. Jesus had taught a wholly new way of organizing and practicing one's religious life: work diligently on changing one's mind, one's basic attitudes; pray in secret, not in public places. There were to be no sacrifices, no rituals, no rules of observance, no rules of cleanness, no priests, and no hierarchies. The Christian religion, so understood, did not resemble any other religion existing in the world known to the early Christians.

At the outset, as we can see from the epistles of Paul and the early chapters of the Acts of the Apostles, the earliest Christian communities preached and practiced the teachings of Jesus. As the Christian Church expanded, however, it welcomed into its communities faithful Jews and devout gentiles who brought with them some of the customs and practices of their former religions. In response to these influences and to the pressures of its historical circumstances, and in the absence of any guidance from Jesus about how to organize and structure his church, the early Christian Church gradually and almost imperceptibly absorbed more and more systems and practices of the Jewish and pagan religions: that is, more and more characteristics of the culture of sacrifice. How this began, and how it continued over the last two thousand years, is the subject of this chapter.

The Original Christian Communities.

St. Paul wrote seven epistles, perhaps more. Some of what he wrote is obscure, and some of his statements seem to contradict others, as he addressed particular problems of the communities to which he wrote. He was certainly the most profound and creative as well as the most energetic of the early Christian writers, and his epistles tell us much about the early beliefs and practices of the first Christians.

Paul taught Jesus's absolute renunciation of violence, with a little touch of Pauline acidity:

> "Do not repay anyone evil for evil, but take thought for what is noble in the sight of all. If it is possible, so far as it depends on you, live peaceably with all. Beloved, never avenge yourselves, but leave room for the wrath of God; for it is written, 'Vengeance is mine, I will repay, says the Lord.' No, if your enemies are hungry, feed them; if they are thirsty, give them something to drink; for by doing this you will heap burning coals on their heads." Rom 12, 17-20.

Paul taught the key Christian virtue of non-judging. In Chapter 14 of Romans, he taught the most careful and sensitive tolerance for the religious practices of others, particularly in matters of dietary observance:

> "Some believe in eating anything, while the weak eat only vegetables. Those who eat must not despise those who abstain, and those who abstain must not pass judgment on those who eat; for God has welcomed them. Who are you to pass judgment on servants of another? It is before their own lord that they stand or fall. And they will be upheld, for the Lord is able to make them stand. . . . Let us therefore no longer pass judgment on one another, but resolve instead never to put a stumbling block or hindrance in the way of another." Rom 14, 2-4, 13.

Paul's teaching was particularly strong on the point of the essential equality of all Christians and of all people. He repeatedly urged Christians to resist the temptation to set up hierarchies or dominant-submissive relationships. "There is no longer Jew or Greek, there is no longer slave or free, there is no longer male or female; for all of you are one in Christ Jesus." Gal 3, 28. In Chapter 12 of 1 Corinthians, Paul compares the various gifts of the Holy Spirit and the varieties of activities within the Christian community to the various organs of the human body:

> "As it is, there are many members, yet one body. The eye cannot say to the hand, 'I have no need of you,' nor again the head to the feet, 'I have no need of you.' On the contrary, the members of the body that seem to be weaker are indispensable, and those members of the body that we think less honorable we clothe with greater honor, and our less respectable members are treated with greater respect; whereas our more respectable members do not need this. But God has so arranged the body, giving the greater honor to the inferior member, that there may be

no dissension within the body, but the members may have the same care for one another. If one member suffers, all suffer together with it; if one member is honored, all rejoice together with it." 1 Cor 12, 20-26.

Paul did not preach the abolition of slavery, perhaps because he thought it a practical impossibility, perhaps because Jesus never directly spoke about slavery, and perhaps because in light of the second coming of Jesus, which he expected soon, he thought of slavery as a temporary condition. Paul said, "Were you a slave when called? Do not be concerned about it. Even if you can gain your freedom, make use of your present condition now more than ever. For whoever was called in the Lord as a slave is a freed person belonging to the Lord, just as whoever was free when called is a slave of Christ." 1 Cor 7, 21-22.

Paul taught Jesus's rejection of petty religious observances: "I know and am persuaded in the Lord Jesus that nothing is unclean in itself; but it is unclean for anyone who thinks it unclean." Rom 14, 14. On another occasion, Paul reproached the Galatians for backsliding into the observance of holy times and days:

"Formerly, when you did not know God, you were enslaved to beings that by nature are not gods. Now, however, that you have come to know God, how can you turn back to the weak and beggarly elemental spirits? How can you want to be enslaved to them again? *You are observing special days, and months, and seasons, and years.* I am afraid that my work for you may have been wasted." Gal 4, 8-11.

How often since then have Christians been instructed *not* to observe "special days, and months, and seasons, and years"?

In the New Testament, there are no Christian priests. The Dominican theologian Yves Congar explains this with precision:

"Here are the facts. The word *hiereus* (priest, sacrificer) appears more than thirty times in the New Testament, and the word *archiereus* more than one hundred and thirty times. The use of these words is so constant that it clearly shows a deliberate and highly significant intention, especially as the writers of the first Christian generations very carefully follow the same line. With them, as with the New Testament, *hiereus* (or *archiereus*) is used to denote either the priests of the levitical order or the pagan priests. Applied to the Christian religion, the word *hiereus* is used only in speaking of Christ or of the faithful. It is never applied to the ministers of the Church's hierarchy."[1]

Paul describes the eucharistic meal of the Corinthians as their regular practice when they "come together as a church." 1 Cor 11, 17-34. The original Christian custom was to celebrate the Lord's supper in their homes, pronounce the words of consecration (1 Cor 11, 23-26), and take communion together, all without the presence of ordained clergy. Acts 2, 42, 46.

In the New Testament, apostles are the Christian missionaries. The original Twelve (commonly called the twelve apostles) were an entirely different group. The scripture scholar Raymond Brown says that "according to New Testament thought there can be no successors to the Twelve as such. . . . Furthermore they cannot be replaced because, precisely as the Twelve, they have an eschatological role to play: in the judgment scene they have been appointed to sit on twelve thrones judging the twelve tribes of Israel (Lk 22, 30; Mt 19, 28)."[2] Of the Twelve, only Peter is reported in the New Testament to have ever left Jerusalem.

But there were many Christian missionary apostles. One (at least) of these was a woman. Paul refers to Junia as "prominent among the apostles." Rom 16, 7. In the New Testament, women were as active as men in the leadership of the Christian Church. The Acts of the Apostles records an occasion where Priscilla and her husband Aquila properly corrected an over-enthusiastic male preacher. Acts 18, 26. Paul tells us not only that many other apostles traveled together as married couples, but that they had the right to do so. Paul rather wistfully asked, "Do not I have the right to be accompanied by a believing wife, as do the other apostles and the brothers of the Lord and Peter?" 1 Cor 9, 5. In Chapter 16 of Romans, Paul sends special greetings to about thirty workers in the Lord; nearly half are women.

Against the custom of his time, Paul spoke quite strongly about the equality that should prevail between men and women. He wrote very carefully, with conscious parallelism:

> "The husband should give to his wife her conjugal rights, and likewise the wife to her husband. For the wife does not have authority over her own body, but the husband does; likewise the husband does not have authority over his own body, but the wife does." 1 Cor 7, 3-4.

> "To the married I give this command—not I but the Lord—that the wife should not separate from her husband (but if she does separate, let her remain unmarried or else be reconciled to her husband), and that the husband should not divorce his wife. To the rest I say—I and not the Lord— that if any believer has a wife who is an unbeliever, and she consents to live with him, he should not divorce her. And if any woman has a husband who is an unbeliever, and he consents to live with her, she should not divorce him. For the unbelieving husband is made holy through his wife, and the unbelieving wife is made holy through her husband. . . . Wife, for all you know, you might save your husband. Husband, for all you know, you might save your wife." 1 Cor 7, 10-16.

In a passage consistent with the Kingdom explanation of the mission of Jesus, Paul implies that the mission of Jesus was to complete the work of God's creation:

> "If creation is full of expectancy, that is because it is waiting for the sons of God to be made known. Created nature has

been condemned to frustration; *not for some deliberate fault of its own,* but for the sake of him who so condemned it, with a hope to look forward to; namely, that nature in its term will be set free from the tyranny of corruption, to share in the glorious freedom of God's sons." Rom 8, 19-21.

The Growing Influence
of the Culture of Sacrifice.

The pull of tradition and custom and the influence of other religions were too strong for nascent Christianity to resist. The earliest departure from Jesus's teachings about the equality of all people before God was the reintroduction of the submission of women. The author of Ephesians writes:

> "Wives, be subject to your husbands as you are to the Lord. For the husband is the head of the wife just as Christ is the head of the church, the body of which he is the Savior. Just as the church is subject to Christ, so also wives ought to be, in everything, to their husbands." Eph 5, 22-24. (Compare this with Eph 6, 5-6: "Slaves, obey your earthly masters with fear and trembling, in singleness of heart, as you obey Christ; not only while being watched, and in order to please them, but as slaves of Christ, doing the will of God from the heart.")

An almost identical passage is found in Colossians 3, 18-19, 22-24, and the teaching is repeated in 1 Tim 2, 11-12; 6, 1-2. The teaching is contrary to the teachings of Jesus, and instead reintroduces classic dominant-submissive behavior, a pattern of the culture of sacrifice.

The better scholarly opinion is that Paul himself did not write Ephesians, Colossians, 2 Thessalonians, 1 Timothy, 2 Timothy and Titus.[3] (If this is the case, they were written by followers of Paul, and still represent very early Christian writing.) For this reason scholars have argued that the passage at 1 Cor 14,

34-35 ("As in all the churches of the saints, women should be
silent in the churches. For they are not permitted to speak, but
should be subordinate, as the law also says.") was added later by
an author other than Paul.[4] Whoever wrote it, this passage indicates
that the rule was adopted from Jewish practice, as set forth in the
Law, which to Paul always means the rules of Judaism. The result
was that, as Garry Wills observed, "A misogyny out of keeping
with the original gospel was absorbed by the church as it acquired
new disciplines and structure."[5]

From its earliest days, the Christian Church preached the
continuity of its teachings with the teachings of the Old
Testament. Peter's first sermon on Pentecost taught that Jesus
was the Messiah foreseen by the Jewish prophets. Acts 2, 14-36.
The earliest Christian communities continued to find prophecies
in the Old Testament which they believed Jesus had fulfilled, so
as to persuade Jews that Jesus was the prophesied Messiah. One
such prophecy is the "suffering servant" prophecy of Isaiah, familiar
to all of us who know Handel's *Messiah*. The following is the
familiar language of the King James version:

> "He is despised and rejected of men; a man of sorrows and
> acquainted with grief . . . . Surely he hath borne our griefs,
> and carried our sorrows: yet we did esteem him stricken,
> smitten of God, and afflicted. But he was wounded for
> our transgressions, he was bruised for our iniquities; the
> chastisement of our peace was upon him; and with his
> stripes we are healed. All we like sheep have gone astray;
> we have turned everyone to his own way; and the Lord
> hath laid on him the iniquity of us all. . . . He was cut off
> out of the land of the living: for the transgression of my
> people was he stricken. . . . Yet it pleased the Lord to bruise
> him; he hath put him to grief . . . . And he bare the sin of
> many, and made intercession for the transgressors." Isaiah
> 53, 3-12.

This truly states the doctrine of substitutionary atonement, and the acts of a brutal God: "It pleased the Lord to bruise him," or (from the Jerusalem Bible), "Yahweh has been pleased to crush him with suffering." But, as we saw in Chapter III, the Old Testament in general and Isaiah in particular contain a mixture of pagan and Christian elements. They often describe a pagan, brutal and vengeful God, as Isaiah does here. In its mission to the Jews, the early Christian Church cast aside the repeated teachings of Jesus about his Father, and absorbed the Jewish brutal and wrathful God.

The idea that Jesus was a sacrificial victim was only indirectly referred to by Paul, as when he said: "Christ our Passover is sacrificed for us. Therefore, let us keep the feast." 1 Cor 5, 8. In the Epistle to the Hebrews, written by a wholly unknown author, the concept of Jesus as sacrificing priest *and* sacrificial victim is fully developed. In the first few centuries of the Christian Church, the pagan idea that Jesus came to offer a blood sacrifice to God was adopted by the Church, and those parts of his teachings which showed that he had come to put an end to sacrifice were not developed.

It was in the early Christian centuries that the idea of Jesus as sacrificial victim was combined with the Lord's Supper. It is a fundamentally pagan idea that true sacrifice must be ritually repeated. This pagan concept worked its way into early Christianity despite the teaching of Hebrews itself, which says that Jesus "has no need to offer sacrifices day after day, first for his own sins, and then for those of the people; this he did once for all when he offered himself." Heb 7, 27. The eucharistic meal was reinterpreted to be a reenactment of the original "sacrificial" death of Jesus, and became the Sacrifice of the Mass.[6]

Once the Lord's Supper had become a sacrificial ritual, it became necessary to have priests, set apart from and above the people of God, to preside at and perform the sacrifice, because "it is the very function of the priest to offer gift and sacrifice." Heb 8, 3. And it became necessary to have bishops, with the power to ordain and anoint priests and confer on them the power to offer sacrifice. Thus hierarchy, and a dominant-submissive class system, became established in the Christian Church by the third century A.D.

In keeping with the tradition of the culture of sacrifice, the priesthood and the hierarchy was reserved to men. Garry Wills has explained the historical justifications given for this exclusion:

> "There were, over the centuries, only two reasons given for excluding women from the priesthood—that they were inferior beings unworthy to hold that dignity, and that their ritual impurity kept them from the altar. The first argument came mainly from pagan antiquity, the second from Jewish temple practice. . . . Thomas Aquinas was not a lone voice but the articulator of a consensus, when he gave the primary motive for refusing ordination to women: 'Since any supremacy of rank cannot be expressed in the female sex, which has the status of an inferior, that sex cannot receive ordination.'"[7]

So dominant-submissive relationships between priest and people and between men and women, both contrary to the express teachings of Jesus, were both adopted by the Christian Church.

The Roman Empire was filled with innumerable sects, cults, local deities, philosophies, theologies and mystery cults of every kind. Christianity was a missionary religion, engaged in trying to persuade others of the truth of its beliefs, in contrast to Judaism and paganism, which were traditional religions, with settled adherents. Christians needed to be able to describe their beliefs and contrast them with those of others, and thus needed to develop tests of what was correct Christian teaching and what was not. From the earliest days, Christianity presented itself (properly, in my view) as a reasonable and internally consistent body of truth, in contrast to nearly all of its competitors. As Keith Hopkins describes it: "Orthodox Christian theology required logical coherence and fine epistemological distinctions; Gnostic visionaries (or their hearers) threaded their way, instead, through a maze of mystical elaborations."[8] The Christian Church survived and grew in its first three centuries by developing three principal institutions: an orthodox statement of faith, a closed definitive canon of scripture, and the teaching authority of the bishops. Power in the Christian Church had necessarily flowed to those who could read, write, preach and argue, which, in days when literacy was relatively rare, was a small minority, the bishops and clerics, further enhancing the dominance of the hierarchy and clergy.

The Establishment of the Church.

The early Christian Church was persecuted here and there throughout the Roman Empire for the first three centuries, but for the first two centuries only on a small scale, spasmodically and locally. From the middle of the third century, the scale of persecutions increased dramatically. The number of Christians had so grown that they were seen as a danger to the Empire, and in 250, 257 and 303 the Roman government launched three successive, large-scale and systematic persecutions targeted at Christian leaders and church property.[9] All of this changed abruptly, within the space of a single generation, under the reign of the emperor Constantine (306-337). Constantine ended the Great Persecution in 312, promulgated a general Edict on Religious Toleration in 313, and himself converted to Christianity in or about 319. Within Constantine's reign, the Christian Church went from the most persecuted sect to the official religion of the Roman Empire.

The establishment of the Christian Church was both a blessing and a curse for the Church and for the lives of Christians. It was obviously a blessing, since it ended the persecutions of Christians from which so many had suffered, and it allowed Christians to take part in the economic and political life of the Roman Empire. It was less obviously but more profoundly a curse.

In the culture of sacrifice, religion is an arm of government. Prohibitions and taboos of the religion must coordinate with the civil government's control and direction of violence through the army and the criminal justice system. Definitions of who is orthodox and who is a non-believer or heretic have political implications. Suspicion and rejection of strangers must be focused on enemies of the state. The mythology of the religion must serve as the unifying and disciplining mythology of the nation or empire. A hierarchical religious command structure will be able to coordinate activities more smoothly with a hierarchical civil government. Indeed, the distinction between state and religion was never in those times seen in the way we see it today.

As the official church of the Roman Empire, the Christian Church became subject to the Roman emperor in many significant ways. Constantine needed unity. He called the bishops of the church to the Council of Nicaea in 325, and he dictated the results of that Council, one of which was the establishment of the Nicene Creed. Before the end of the fourth century, heresy was defined as a capital crime by the emperor Theodosius (379-395).

As we saw in Chapter VII, Jesus's death and resurrection had effectively eliminated the institution of ritual blood sacrifice from the civilized world. After Jesus's death, it was no longer possible to see the sacrificial victim as the one who is guilty of the crimes of the people; the necessary psychological transference could no longer be made. But the human instinct to transfer guilt to another found a substitute for sacrifice in the persecution of outsiders or outsider groups. It was still possible, and very human, for a people to believe that the source of their troubles, and the cause of God's displeasure, was the presence of unbelieving outsiders in the midst of the community: the heretics, the unbelievers, the Jews. Christian people could believe this, transfer the guilt and blame to the Others, and persecute them. So medieval Christians could really believe that the Jews had caused the plague; seventeenth-century Christians could really believe that the women they identified as witches were in league with the devil; and Southern white men in the late nineteenth and early twentieth century America could really believe that the African Americans whom they lynched were to blame for their own fate and deserved their cruel deaths. This cultural adaptation of the institution of sacrifice is morally more repugnant than the random and arbitrary selection of a victim which it replaced. Yet it began as soon as Christians were free of persecutions themselves, and grew over the ages to horrific proportions.

The Christian Church in the Dark Ages.

During the fourth through tenth centuries, the Christian Church absorbed a great many pagans as new members, first from within the empire and later from the conversion of the Northern European barbarian nations. It was impossible to convert all the inherited pagan practices (rituals, sacred objects, sacred places, feast days, observances and superstitions) of the newly-baptized Christians directly to Jesus's ideal of an interior devotion and private prayer to God. The best that could be done was to develop Christian rituals, fast and feast days, devotions to saints and to relics of saints, and rules of sexual morality and ritual cleanness which could be substituted for their pagan counterparts. So another portion of Jesus's rejection of the religious practices of the culture of sacrifice was lost, and the practices of the Christian Church came more and more to resemble those of its pagan forebears.

The barbarian tribal kingdoms of Northern France, Britain and Scandinavia were social and religious kingdoms of the culture of sacrifice. As Christopher Dawson describes them,

> "This archaic type of tribal kingdom derived its stability not from the power and authority of the ruler but from its own specific gravity and from the complex network of kinship and inherited status which held the people together in a community the structure of which was consecrated by religion and sacred tradition. And the king was the natural centre in which all these traditions and loyalties were concentrated. He was the embodiment of the life of the nation and the life of the land. He was the representative

of the people to the gods as high priest, who presided at
the sacrifices, and he represented the gods to the people
by virtue of his divine ancestry and the sacred prestige of
his blood and his office."[10]

The conversion of such a king to Christianity effected the
conversion of his people. But the king remained the high priest
and sacred warrior, and the Christianity of the converted people
remained pagan in many fundamental respects.

The new empire of Charlemagne (about 800 A.D.) formed
a unitary church-state under the emperor, the divinely-appointed
leader of the Christian people. The Carolingian empire embodied
a kind of theocratic constitutionalism which greatly influenced
the development of European monarchies.[11] Church and state
were bound together, but with two sources of authority and power,
the king and the Pope.

The great institution of Christian monasticism, founded in
the waning years of the Roman Empire, first the Irish version
and then the Benedictine version, was critical for the survival of
the Christian Church and the preservation of classical culture
through the Dark Ages. The independence, decentralization and
stability of monastic life gave it the power to survive the barbarian
invasions of that period. From the Irish monasteries came many
of the missionaries who converted the northern European rulers
and their people to Christianity.[12] The rules of the monasteries
required the monks to practice the attitude-changing virtues which
Jesus taught, non-violence, non-judging, forgiveness, humility,
and detachment from possessions, assisted by the vows of poverty,
chastity, obedience and stability. But while these Christian virtues
were thus preserved and practiced, they were practiced in a
cloistered world apart, not in the everyday world in which Jesus
had expected them to act as a leaven for the whole people.

Monasticism also fostered the growth of penitential forms
of piety, with emphasis on frequent and detailed examinations
of conscience, many small and specific rules and observances,
and a preoccupation with sexual morality and ritual cleanness.

This emphasis, still present in many Christian Churches, runs counter to the teaching of Jesus that his followers should be more concerned with changing basic dispositions and instinctive habits than with scrupulously observing rules.

There was an amazing growth of the monastic movement in size and influence through the Dark Ages, particularly in the ninth and tenth centuries. Because of the stability of the monastic culture in those unstable times, many monks were relatively well-educated and disciplined, compared to the secular clergy, and rose to high levels in the Church. During the same period, the Church continued to increase the requirements of ritual purity for priests who offered the Sacrifice of the Mass. These two factors persuaded the Roman Popes that clerical celibacy would be a good thing for the whole Church, and clerical celibacy was imposed by Rome on all clergy in the eleventh century.

The Christian Church in the High Middle Ages.

After Rome fell, Christianity was the only surviving cultural force in the West. For centuries, virtually the only people who could read and write were clerics and monks. Since men who could read and write were indispensable to the administration of civil government, clerics and monks staffed all the centers of civil administration, such as they were. This led to a major unsought growth in the temporal power of many bishops, abbots, priests and monks. By the tenth century, most of Germany and many portions of France consisted of clerical principalities, ruled by bishops. The central portion of Italy, the Papal States, was ruled by the Bishop of Rome, now the Pope. Bishops in the early Christian era had, more often than not, been selected by election by the people of the local diocese. By the Early Middle Ages the union of church and state and the growing secular power of bishops had made it impossible for rulers of church or state to permit popular election of bishops. Kings of the nascent European nations needed the loyalty of the local rulers within their domains, frequently appointed their own relatives and loyal followers as bishops and abbots, and fought tenaciously with Rome for the continued power to appoint bishops within their own countries. This struggle over lay investiture continued throughout the Middle Ages.

By the end of the first millennium, the Bishop of Rome had achieved primacy of rule over the Western Christian Church, a role which the Popes still claim. The rise of the Popes to power was aided considerably by astute papal politics, by the political independence of the Papal States with Rome as the center, and by the dissemination in the eighth and ninth centuries of numerous critical forged documents purporting to support the Popes' claims to primacy over the entire Christian Church.[13] With the great papal reforms of the eleventh century, initiated by German kings, and continued under Popes Leo IX (1049-54) and Gregory VII (1067-80), papal supremacy became a practical and potent political force. Gregory VII asserted that the Pope had the power to depose kings, and he proved it against Henry IV of Germany at Canossa in 1077. To obey God now meant to obey the Pope, and vice versa. As Hans Küng states it, "From this time [the time of Gregory VII] the obedience of all Christians is a central virtue for Rome, and to give orders and compel obedience (by whatever means) is the Roman style."[14] The Pope even asserted claims to infallibility. Gregory VII wrote that "The Roman church has never erred, and according to the testimony of scripture will never ever err." Gregory VII was the first Pope to grant indulgences to Christians for waging offensive war. The church of Christ had now become a centralized, legalistic, political, military and clerical power.[15]

Let us examine the state of the Christian Church in the High Middle Ages, roughly from 1070 to 1280. To be sure, there were holy men and women living by the teachings of Jesus during this period, as there have been in all ages of the Christian era. But we need to consider the culture of the institution of the Christian Church as such.

The Christian Church of that period was a violent and militant church. The Pope ruled central Italy and had his own army. In 1095 Pope Urban II preached the first of eight Crusades against the Muslims who had occupied the land of Palestine. He thus used the power and authority of the papacy to begin and prosecute an aggressive war of conquest. In 1209, Pope Innocent III directed the king of France to wage war upon the Cathar heretics in southwestern France. The French King obliged with a ruthless and bloody massacre of a whole population.[16] To eradicate the remaining heretics, Innocent III established the Roman Inquisition in 1215, and in 1254 his successor Innocent IV, himself an Inquisitor, authorized the Inquisition to use torture to aid its inquiries. During this entire period Christians persecuted Jews throughout Christendom.[17]

As Joseph Kelly explains, during the High Middle Ages "for most Europeans, evil manifested itself in the Other, the person who differed from the dominant views of society."[18] Included among the "Others" were Muslims, Jews, heretics and women. With few exceptions, the power of the Christian Church was used to reduce the Others to submission, and to transfer blame to the Others for the problems of the people.

The institutional Christian Church was hierarchical in the extreme, with all power and authority concentrated in the clerical establishment and all final authority reserved to the Pope. It was wealthy and acquisitive; the corruption of the papal court and the rapacity of its levies for the expenses of the papacy in the Later Middle Ages was a major cause of the Protestant Reformation.

The early Christian institution of the Lord's Supper had been replaced by the Mass, an attenuated form of sacrifice. It was celebrated by the priest in Latin, then as now a foreign language to most lay Christians, with his back to the people. In many large churches and cathedrals, the rood screen entirely separated the celebrant and the choir from the congregation. Christianity to the lay people was a religion of feasts and fasts, of small rules and observances, of holy places to which one went on pilgrimage, and of holy things like golden monstrances and chalices and relics of all sorts. In short, the Christian Church was the complete model of a church of the culture of sacrifice. It was at this time that Anselm wrote his explanation of the mission of Jesus and his redeeming sacrifice in substitutionary atonement for the sins of mankind. It is not surprising that his explanation includes a wrathful God who demands and is pleased by the torture and death of his only Son; this is a pure culture of sacrifice explanation from a Church wholly overtaken by the culture of sacrifice.

How could such a Christian Church teach the core teachings of Jesus? How could a Church in which a fully-armored Renaissance Pope personally led his army to battle on horseback teach absolute non-violence? How could the Church of the Crusades and the Inquisition teach tolerance, non-judging and forgiveness? How could the Renaissance Church of the Medicis and the Borgias teach detachment from possessions? How could the Church of Innocent III and Boniface VIII[19] preach an end to hierarchical and dominant-submissive relationships? It couldn't. As Kelly observes,

> "In Early Christianity heresy usually took the form of intellectual dissent from official teaching. In the High Middle Ages, intellectual heresy continued but it was more and more replaced by social heresies, that is, heresies which excoriated the official Church for not living up to its proclaimed ideals."[20]

The Christian Church defended itself by persecuting as heretics those who saw the differences between the practices of the Church and the teachings of Jesus.

What is surprising about all of this to the modern observer is how little the Christian Churches have changed since the High Middle Ages. The culture of sacrifice has enormous survival power. Power does what it does to preserve itself. Most of the changes in the Christian Churches which have taken place since the High Middle Ages have been forced on them from outside. Let us now examine some of those changes.

Failed Reform.

Pressures for reform of a corrupt papacy and a corrupt clergy in the Late Middle Ages culminated in the reform movement led by Martin Luther in Germany, beginning in 1517. Luther, an Augustinian monk, was profoundly rooted in Augustinian teachings, principally those of predestination, the corruption of mankind, and grace as God's pure favor, manifest in Jesus. Luther preached a radical return to the gospel of Jesus: Scripture only, Christ only, grace only, and faith only. The Christian Church was to be the universal priesthood of believers, and the Holy Eucharist a sign of faith, not a sacrifice. These reforms were sorely needed, but only partially realized. The Protestant Reformation spread through northern Europe, but was not able to maintain unity. Countless reforming sects with differing programs warred with each other. Within a few generations, each local ruler in Germany had determined the acceptable religion for his principality, and each used the power of the state to enforce adherence to his choice. *Cujus regio, ejus religio* ("Whoever rules, we follow his religion") was the rule. This is a perfect rule of the culture of sacrifice, and wholly inconsistent with the freedom of conscience sought and taught by Jesus. Calvinism, which spread from Geneva, was also compulsory wherever it was adopted. Dissenters were faced with inquisition, torture and death at the hands of the secular government.

By the end of the sixteenth century, each branch of Protestant Christianity had its "confession," a statement of its principles of faith and its social discipline, to be enforced by church and state, and the period of reform was closed. Basic to most Protestant denominations was the replacement of the teaching authority of the Christian Church with the acceptance of the literal inerrancy of scripture. The divisions among the "confessions" were major factors in the Wars of Religion (late 16th century), the Thirty Years War (1618-48), and the English Civil War (1642-60), which devastated France, Germany and England respectively until the contending parties sank in mutual exhaustion.

Despite the initial efforts of the Protestant reformers to

remove the notion of sacrifice from the eucharistic ritual of the church, the Protestant Churches accepted most of the principles and practices of the culture of sacrifice, while the Roman Catholic Church retained them. One evidence of the continuing power of the culture of sacrifice over the Christian Churches is the lamentable fact that, in the sixteenth and seventeenth centuries, both Catholics and Protestants throughout Europe engaged in repeated and widespread witch hunts, trials and executions. People of a town or village would experience misfortune, whether from war, plague or death in the family. In classic culture of sacrifice fashion, first one, then another, and then all would blame their troubles on an outcast, usually a poor widow, and transfer responsibility and guilt to her, blaming the accidents of misfortune on her curses and her supposed league with the devil. Both church authorities and the secular judicial system often supported the accusations of all against one, and many of the accused were convicted and punished.[21] It is estimated that over one hundred thousand persons, eighty to ninety percent of whom were women, were executed for witchcraft during that period. One historian writes that "With the exception of the persecutions of the Jews, these trials led to the greatest mass killing of human beings by other human beings in Europe which were not the result of war."[22] The witch hunt craze spread even to the isolated new world, in Salem, Massachusetts in 1692. This was a manifestation of the continued pernicious powers of the culture of sacrifice in Christian communities on a large scale.

The Modern Christian Churches.

By the eighteenth century, both the Roman Catholic Church and the reformed Protestant Churches had lost most, if not all, of their influence on culture and history, not to speak of science and philosophy. The eighteenth century Enlightenment brought to Europe and America a new secular faith in reason, in the knowability of nature, and in the inevitability of progress. Political philosophers of the Enlightenment resurrected, as secular philosophical virtues, some fundamental Christian values.

Jesus's teachings that all men are called to the Kingdom of Heaven, that he came to call sinners, not the just, that the first shall be last and the last shall be first, and that hierarchical and dominant-submissive relationships should end, were reborn in Jefferson's revolutionary words, "We hold these truths to be self-evident, that all men are created equal." Jesus's teaching of non-judging, which I understand to require at least a tolerance and respect for the opinions of others, became the separation of church and state, the freedoms of speech, of the press and of assembly, and the freedom of religious exercise embodied in the First Amendment to the United States Constitution. In their own way, the earliest Christian communities had lived by the virtues of liberty, equality and fraternity. These values had been overlaid by the dogmatism of the Hellenistic Christian Church and by the hierarchical command structure of the medieval Christian Church, and had been only partially restored in the Protestant Reformation. When liberty, equality and fraternity emerged in the American Revolution, and more so in the French Revolution, they were not recognized as Christian virtues, and were bitterly resisted by the Roman Catholic Church.

In the nineteenth century, the Roman Catholic Church turned even more sharply away from the modern era. Pope Pius IX, Pope from 1846 to 1873, recently beatified by Pope John Paul II, led the march to the past:

(a) In 1864 he issued an encyclical, *Quanta Cura*, to which was attached a Syllabus of Modern Errors, a wholesale condemnation of all modern ideas, including among them "that erroneous opinion which is especially injurious to the Catholic Church and the salvation of souls, called by our predecessor Gregory XVI insane raving, namely, that freedom of conscience and of worship is the proper right of each man, and that this should be proclaimed and asserted in every rightly constituted society."[23]

(b) In 1850 he defined the doctrine of the Immaculate Conception of Mary, a doctrine wholly without scriptural support. This increased the Roman Catholic emphasis on the role of Mary in the redemption of humanity, and indirectly confirmed the remoteness of the human Jesus and of his teachings from the teachings of the Roman Catholic Church.

(c) In 1870, with the First Vatican Council, he formally established the doctrine of the infallibility of the Pope, a doctrine which is on the historical record demonstrably untrue,[24] and which has had the practical effect of paralyzing Popes and bishops of the Roman Catholic Church from making any changes, because any change would involve the admission of previous error, and the doctrine says this cannot occur.

In the twentieth century, the promise of reform of the Roman Catholic Church which was given at the Council of Vatican II failed, and the Roman Catholic Church has again resolutely set its face against reform. In the Protestant Churches, many of the most active movements of the last two centuries have been evangelical or fundamentalist in nature, which have included a strong reliance on the literal inspiration and unconditional inerrancy of scripture, opposition to all of modern science and philosophy, and hostility to much theology as well.

With all the good in the lives of their individual members, institutional Christian Churches have remained bound by the culture of sacrifice. The voice of Jesus calling for non-violence was seldom heard during the centuries of warfare in Europe and in the new world. The Christian Churches had retreated behind "confessional" walls and judged and condemned every one outside the walls. The Christian Churches have remained dominated by clerics and preachers, and filled with detailed rituals and rules of prohibition and observance. There continues a strong and repeatedly displayed tendency of Christians, both Catholic and Protestant, with the leadership of their clerics and preachers, to seek to impose and enforce their own particular moral rules on a society which does not accept them, not by persuasion, but rather by legal compulsion (the good old Roman way). Illustrations of this are the Prohibition movement in the early decades of the last century and the anti-abortion movement of the last few decades. The German philosopher Max Horkheimer succinctly expressed the present distance between Jesus and the Christian Churches: "Anyone who does not see from the Gospel that Jesus died in opposition to his modern representatives is unable to read."[25]

The Christian Churches, so thoroughly penetrated with values of the culture of sacrifice, have generally been unable or unwilling to preach the teachings of Jesus which are subversive of the culture of sacrifice. As a result, the image of Jesus generally held by Christians of our age is a meek and mild Jesus who bears little or no resemblance to the Jesus found in the Gospels. Douglas John Hall describes this image as follows:

> "We begin by turning once again to the scriptural witness to Jesus. This is where all Christology that intends to be faithful to the *sola Scriptura* of the Reformation must begin, and there is perhaps no branch of the ecumenical church that is more in need of such a beginning today than is Protestantism. For the impression is far too easily maintained within this camp, with its deliberate emphasis on the Bible, that its dearly held preconceptions about the Christ are true because they are (naturally) 'biblical.' It is too little realized that within the broadly Protestant fold, 'biblical' regularly stands for long-established conventions that, while they might have had their origins in Scripture, have become so stylized and sterile that they no longer challenge the church but may be treated as possessions—familiar patterns of belief so predictable as to contain no element either of surprise, offense, or wonder.

"Thus Jesus, for perhaps the vast majority of Euro-American Protestants in North America, is a good, mild-mannered, sexless, kindly but serious, nonpolitical male of indeterminate age, who counsels devotion to God, evenness of temper, patient acceptance of difficult experiences, courtesy in one's dealings with others, obedience to those in authority, and resignation with cheerfulness in the face of sickness and death. This Jesus, in short, looks much like a white Anglo-Saxon Protestant, also in his implicit but decisive renunciation of any Jewish traits, and he behaves in a way that is quite unlikely to throw into question any of the mores, taboos, and values governing mainstream culture. And those who carry about such a mental image of the Christ can do so, being Protestants, in the firm belief that it is entirely biblical."[26]

I would add to Hall's description only that in my view he very accurately describes the image of Jesus held by most North American Roman Catholics as well.

I have proposed that Jesus came to overcome the culture of sacrifice, and replace it with the culture of the Kingdom of Heaven. If Christians had listened to the teachings of Jesus and had resisted the influence of the culture of sacrifice over the last two millennia, the Christian Churches would now be far different institutions, and Christian life would be lived in an entirely different light. What is needed is a new understanding of Jesus's mission, a new grasp of and adherence to his core teachings, and a return to the principles and practices of the Christian communities of the first generation, before the Christian Church began to absorb practices of the culture of sacrifice. In the next and final chapter, I will try to describe what the life of a Christian should be in the light of the Kingdom explanation of the mission of Jesus.

Notes:

1. Congar, Yves, O.P., *Priest and Layman*, pp. 74-75, quoted in Wills, Garry, *Papal Sin: Structures of Deceit* (Doubleday, 2000), p. 110.

2. Brown, Raymond E., S.S., *Priest and Bishop: Biblical Reflections* (Paulist Press, 1970), p. 55.

3. Barrett, C. K., *Paul: An Introduction to His Thought* (Westminster/John Knox Press, 1994), pp. 3-5.

4. Wills, *op. cit.*, p. 121, n. 56.

5. Wills, *op. cit.*, p. 117.

6. Küng, Hans, *Christianity* (Continuum, 1998), pp. 151-52.

7. Wills, *op. cit.*, p. 107.

8. Hopkins, Keith, *A World Full of Gods* (Penguin Putnam, 2001), p. 257.

9. Hopkins, *op. cit.*, p. 110.

10. Dawson, Christopher, *Religion and the Rise of Western Culture* (Doubleday Image Books, 1958), p. 71.

11. Dawson, *op. cit.*, pp. 75-83.

12. Cahill, Thomas, *How the Irish Saved Civilization* (Talese/Doubleday, 1995).

13. Küng, *op. cit.*, pp. 365-72.

14. Küng, *op. cit.*, p. 381.

15. Küng, *op. cit.*, pp. 390-403.

16. O'Shea, Stephen, *The Perfect Heresy* (Walker & Co., 2000).

17. Carroll, James, *Constantine's Sword* (Houghton Mifflin Co., 2001), pp. 246-77.

18. Kelly, Joseph F., *The Problem of Evil in the Western Tradition* (Liturgical Press, 2002), p. 68.

19. Boniface VIII, Pope from 1294 to 1303, asserted his power to demand obedience from Christian kings and people, and defined obedience to the Pope as "utterly necessary for salvation for every human creature." Küng, *op. cit.*, pp. 458-61.

20. Kelly, *op. cit.*, p. 71.

21. Thomas, Keith, *Religion and the Decline of Magic* (Penguin Books, 1973). pp. 638-80.

22. Schorman, *Hexen*, quoted in Küng, *op. cit.*, p. 614.

23. Fiedler, Maureen and Rabben, Linda, ed., *Rome Has Spoken* (Crossroad Publishing, 1998), p. 105.

24. Fiedler and Rabben, *op. cit., passim.*

25. Horkheimer, Max, quoted in Küng, Hans, *Does God Exist? An Answer for Today* (Crossroad Publishing, 1978), p. 325.

26. Hall, Douglas John, *Professing the Faith* (Fortress Press, 1996), p. 485.

IX

CHRISTIAN LIFE UNDER THE KINGDOM EXPLANATION.

What are the implications of the Kingdom explanation for the life of a Christian? How does being a Christian work in the light of this understanding of the core teachings of Jesus and of his renunciation of the culture of sacrifice, the way of the world? I shall examine these questions under four headings:

1. Conversion.
2. Sanctification—The Interior Life.
3. Sanctification—The Christian Community.
4. The Sanctification of the World.

Conversion.

For two thousand years, the story of Jesus's life, his teachings, his death and his resurrection has been passed from generation to generation by word of mouth. Since the story of Jesus was reduced to writing within two generations or so of his death, the oral message received can be checked against the written word, and its authenticity verified. But almost everyone who has heard of Jesus has learned of him from oral teaching, from parents, preachers, priests and teachers, as part of a continuous oral tradition now spanning roughly one hundred generations. This transmission of the Good News is perhaps the most important, and certainly the most fundamental, work of the Christian community, the

Christian Church. There may be individual revelations, as in the case of Paul on the road to Damascus, and certainly Christians believe that God acts in history, as the Holy Spirit, to preserve and extend the teaching of Christ's message and mission, but the ordinary way of human teaching and human learning is almost always the way the story is given and received.

At first, particularly if the recipient is a child, the message is received and accepted as true and normative because of the authority of the teacher. The child believes that his parents, his Sunday school or parochial school teacher, and his priest or preacher, are good people; he sees that they believe the Christian message and that they think that he should believe it too; and so he accepts it as true. Some people are non-reflective either by ability or by inclination, or, after they have reflected to some extent upon the teachings of Christ, find themselves unable to form an independent conviction on the matter. They either remain childlike believers all their lives, or drift away from any inclination toward or interest in Christ's teachings at all. But some people, as they mature in thought and judgment, continue (or resume) reflecting on the teachings of Jesus, and decide to accept his teachings as true, and to accept his redemptive activity for themselves, not on the authority of their parents or teachers, but because they personally judge them to be good and true. This is the event of conversion.

It takes a certain amount of life experience to conclude that one wishes to be a mature Christian, that is, to be converted. One must have spent some time trying to govern one's own conduct, and one must have experienced both the difficulty of doing so and the difficulties other people have had with trying to do the same. One must have studied and reflected upon the teachings of one or more of the Christian Churches to see if they offer the organizing principles and the moral guidance one is seeking. This is just the process of growing up, becoming mature, and deciding how to live one's life as an adult. If a person's self-directed choice is to become a mature Christian, this is called conversion. The mature Christian joins, or continues his membership in, a church or congregation, goes to services regularly, and tries to lead a good life. He or she listens to sermons, reads the bible or other Christian literature, and participates in the life of the Christian community.

But is this the whole meaning of conversion? I don't think so. To be a Christian is to be a follower of Jesus, a person who is trying to change his own mind and put on the mind and heart of Jesus. That means that he or she signs on to the program, and to the teachings, particularly the core teachings, of Jesus. Have most, or many, present-day Christians signed on? Roughly seven out of every ten Americans call themselves Christian. Yet within the week following the destruction of the World Trade Center, ninety-six percent of Americans favored the government's proposed reaction of retributive violence toward those who perpetrated the destruction and all who had aided them. This is a very human and understandable response, but it is clearly the response of the culture of sacrifice. It is the response of the people who follow the "white bread" Jesus described at the end of the last chapter. It is not the response of people who take the Sermon on the Mount seriously.

In the traditional teaching of many Christian Churches, the center of Christianity is that Jesus died for our sins. This was an arrangement between God the Son and God the Father, in which mankind did not really participate, but as a result of Jesus's death we can be saved if we acknowledge him as the one who saved us. To people who have converted to this form of Christianity, the teachings of Jesus are quite secondary. It does not materially affect one's salvation if one distinguishes away the more difficult of these teachings, such as non-violence or forgiveness of one's enemies, as ideals meant only for saints, or as rhetorical exaggerations for emphasis. If a Christian simply continues to trust in Jesus and follow the rules and practices of a Christian Church, then Jesus will take care of him. To such Christians, ignoring the words of Jesus in the Sermon on the Mount is not the best practice, but it's quite acceptable in the circumstances. But if the teachings of Jesus are the most important part of his mission, and if Jesus intends to determine who his followers are by seeing whether they observe his teachings and accept his words (as I believe he said he would do), the answer must be different. Non-violence, non-resistance, and turning the other cheek must be the initial response of the committed Christian.

I suggest, then, that for many Christians, the Kingdom explanation of Jesus's mission, which makes his teachings, particularly his core teachings, the most important part of his mission, presents a call for a real conversion to a quite different version of Christianity. It has presented a call for a real conversion to me, as I have worked out the implications of my views, and it is not an easy call to answer.

The conversion to Jesus's teachings is difficult. Let's not kid ourselves. The hard part of conversion to Jesus and his teachings is not reaching the belief that there is a God, or concluding that the Gospels are reasonably authentic and accurate records of the life and teachings of Jesus, or even believing that Jesus rose from the dead. The hard part is committing oneself to the required change of mind, and deciding to take on the very difficult task of becoming non-violent, non-judging, forgiving, humble and detached from one's possessions. I had a revealing conversation with my legal assistant on September 12, 2002, just after the day of first anniversary observances of the terrorist bombings of September 11. "The hardest Christian doctrine to accept," I suggested, "is that human life survives death." "No," she replied. "The hardest Christian doctrine to accept is non-violence. We want so much to retaliate and get vengeance." I think she was right. The conversion to the change of mind and heart required by Jesus does not require a leap of faith; it requires courage, not a leap of courage, but steadfast courage. And none of us is sure enough in our hearts that we will have steadfast courage. This is why the person of Jesus, and the example of his life, is so important. This is why he did not say that "I have taught you the way, and the truth, and the life," but "I *am* the way, and the truth, and the life." We can reason our way to the correctness of a body of teachings, but we need a leader, and in this case the example of a real human leader who has already traveled the path, to make a commitment of steadfast courage.

In a way, the challenge of Jesus's teachings and his invitation to each of us to join him in the struggle against the "world," the culture of sacrifice, presents us with a dilemma:

(a) On the one hand, life is hard enough. We don't need to go out of our way to find hard things to do. The established pattern of life in the tradition of the Christian Churches is a good life: worship of God, community participation, doing good works, obeying the commandments—that should be enough. The key virtues are moral ideals for saints, not for every man. And yet what is so bland, so comforting, so lacking in vision and idealism, as life in a traditional Christian parish or congregation? And what is so immature as waiting for priests and ministers to tell us what it is to be Christian?

(b) On the other hand, one who makes a commitment to the core teachings of Jesus accepts a great deal of personal responsibility. Such a commitment could easily require a person to take socially unacceptable stands, or to engage in financially unproductive activity. It could make one's life a lot less comfortable, and perhaps more lonely, as so much of the work in changing one's own mind is interior and reflective. But what a thing it would be to decide to commit one's mind and heart to putting on the mind and heart of Jesus in the way he called us to do it!

What of the roles of grace and faith in this process of conversion? There is a tendency in Christian teaching to describe grace as a thing which God gives to men, separate from the gifts of conversion and sanctification, so that the recipient can by the power of grace receive the gifts of conversion and sanctification. In Protestant evangelical theology, the Christian must first receive grace from God before he can accept the revelation of Jesus as his redeemer. Similarly, in Roman Catholic theology, "Faith is a gift of God, a supernatural virtue infused by him. *Before* this faith can be exercised, man must have the grace of God to move and assist him . . . . Believing is possible only by grace and the interior helps of the Holy Spirit."[1] Grace is described as a separate supernatural substance rather than as a simple relationship. In my view, this concept of grace is unnecessary and misleading.

The principal reason this confusing theology of grace was developed was to leave no question that the redemption of men and women by Jesus is the free gift of God, unearned and unmerited by humans. After all, grace is simply another word for gift. But the theology of grace as a separate substance is not needed to protect this teaching. A simpler and more direct way to state the redemptive message is to say that Jesus *is* grace, he *is* the gift of God, for God opened his God-consciousness, and he was united with God in his life, his teaching, his death and his resurrection. Jesus comes to each of us by the natural means of the spoken and written word. Thus is grace transmitted. Each person responds to this gift, this grace, if, as and when he or she accepts the person of Jesus as redeemer and commits to follow and practice his core teachings. Thus is grace received. The act of believing and committing is not based on an infused power separate from the truths the believer believes and from the person to whom the believer commits. The truths the believer believes comprise a set of truths at which the believer has arrived by the natural process of the reasoning intelligent mind. There is no "grace" separate from the message of Jesus itself. There is no "supernatural faith." The believer concludes, based on the evidence, that there was a person called Jesus; that he said what the Gospels record him as having said; that he lived the life the Gospels record him as having lived; and that his call to every man to follow him in leading a life of the key virtues and the core teachings is a call to which one ought to respond affirmatively. This is all perfectly natural. Whether we respond to the call or not is not an act of faith; it is an act of courage.

Let us suppose that a person has decided that he or she wishes to be a follower of Jesus, to study and to learn to practice the core teachings: how should he or she go about it, and what should be the result? Let us consider first the interior work which needs to be done, and the desired and expected effects of that work.

Then we will discuss how a group of such persons would work together in a Christian community, and what such a community might look like. Finally, we will explore together, in a very preliminary way, how people so oriented might effect changes in the world.

Sanctification—The Interior Life.

Jesus assumed, and we can assume, as the foundation upon which we can begin work on developing the key virtues, that we are already habitually practicing the normal good conduct of men and women in a civilized society, observing the natural law or the ten commandments, and the civil law and customs of the time and place. Jesus assumed we would know how to do this and would be trying to do so. Becoming a follower of Jesus requires more than this.

One of the earliest and most direct statements of how to become a follower of Jesus is found in St. Paul's letter to the Phillippians: "Let this mind be in you, which was also in Christ Jesus." Phil 2, 5. The Christian is to absorb the teachings and the life of Jesus into his own consciousness, as normative for his own life. Clearly the place to start is to become truly familiar with Jesus's life and his teachings. This means reading and rereading the Gospels. Good commentary is often helpful and sometimes necessary. Reading other parts of the bible can shed light on the Gospels. But the foundation must be a deep and reflective familiarity with the Gospel texts themselves.

Jesus repeatedly called for prayer, and for praying in secret. I think that what he meant, and what this requires, particularly in light of his call that we change our minds, is reflective thought and affective meditation on his life and words, particularly his words describing the core teachings and key virtues. One way of praying, and the way that is essential here, is turning the teachings of Jesus over and over in our minds, reflecting on how they might be put into practice and how they should be applied in one's own life.

Consider the key external virtues: non-violence, non-judging, forgiveness. At first, these virtues appear to be purely reactive in nature. One can practice non-violence only in a situation in which one is attacked in some way or other. One can practice non-judging only if one is in a situation in which one is tempted to judge, to criticize, or to condemn another. One can forgive only when there is something to forgive. But that is a superficial view. We need to practice the external virtues before the provocation arises, or we'll never be able to control our instinctive genetically-based reactions, when provoked, which are to fight back or hate the offender or both. One of the enduring lessons of the struggle for African American civil rights in the South in the 1960's is that the leaders, long before the sit-ins and protest marches, had studied non-violence, and had led workshops and seminars to teach non-violent protest to their followers.[2] We need to practice the external virtues ahead of the time of need so that a non-violent, non-judging and forgiving reaction to provocation will be deep-seated and instinctive. We can do this practice in prayer and reading, and with the help of others in study groups, seminars, and workshops. The object will be to accustom the mind and the emotions to non-violent, non-judging and forgiving ways of thinking.

Broadening one's intellectual and emotional horizons is generally a good way to develop one's understanding of people and cultures different from one's own, and one's ability imaginatively to cross the barriers of ethnicity, race and language and empathize with others in a non-judging and forgiving way. All of one's education and experience can be oriented toward the development of the key virtues if we choose to use them that way. There is a close connection between first seeing all men and women as similar to us, next resisting violence and judging, and finally learning to follow Jesus's last command to us: that we love one another. Thomas Merton expressed this connection this way:

"Violence rests on the assumption that the enemy and I are entirely different: the enemy is evil and I am good. But love sees things differently. It sees that even the enemy suffers from the same sorrows and limitations that I do. That we both have the same hopes, the same needs, the same aspirations for a peaceful and harmless human life. And that death is the same for both of us."[3]

It will take more progress in seeing things this way than most of us have so far achieved to be able to see that Timothy McVeigh and Mohammad Atta had "the same hopes, the same needs, the same aspirations for a peaceful and harmless human life" as we do. But that is the goal. We know from everything he said that that is how Jesus would have seen it.

Developing the key internal virtues, humility and detachment from possessions, also requires prayerful meditation and careful thinking. But these virtues can also be practiced from day to day in our own lives. Each person will develop highly personal ways of trying to practice these virtues. For me, it is important to remember that Jesus counseled humility most often in the context of one's interior religious life. We must avoid taking pride in our own virtue; we must avoid self-righteousness, historically a prominent characteristic of many otherwise good Christians. Humility should not be hard to practice; each of us has much to be humble about. If you are feeling righteous, reflect on how well you have developed the habitual practice of thinking of people of other races or ethnic groups as your true equals. And for myself, one way to develop and retain some detachment from possessions is to keep before my mind the matters which are so much more important than possessions: love of God, love of family, love of neighbor, and continued work on deepening one's understanding and full acceptance of the teachings of Jesus, not to speak of good music and good literature.

Because each of the key virtues is directly opposed to a naturally-selected antisocial behavior pattern built into our genes, trying to acquire and develop the key virtues requires continued internal wrestling against one's instinctive urges and desires. It is a lifelong task. These virtues are "key" not only in the sense I have discussed, that is, they were specifically and repeatedly taught by Jesus, but in two other ways:

(a) First, the effort to put on the mind of Jesus in the matter of the key virtues spills over into the rest of the life of the follower of Jesus, so that his or her practice of other virtues becomes easier and more habitual. For example, one who works hard at non-judging and spiritual humility will naturally tend to become more patient, more sympathetic to the needs and wants of others, more forgiving, and more kind.

(b) Second, the continued and persistent internal effort to change one's mind, emotions and habitual reactions from our instinctive views and responses to the attitudes and habits of one who is non-violent, non-judging, forgiving, humble and detached from possessions is the highest exercise of human intellect and will in which a man or woman can engage. This activity, it seems to me, is what makes a person mature, self-directed, and most fully human. We would practice these virtues more diligently if we truly understood their power to make each person strong, self-directed, mature and free. In the real world, of course, we would not practice them at all if Jesus had not first taught them and then lived them. The effect on one's life and character which comes with cultivation of the key virtues is what Jesus meant to tell us when he said, "If you continue in the word, you are truly my disciples; and you will know the truth, *and the truth will make you free.*" Jn 8, 31-32.

If we put on the habits and attitudes of the key virtues, then, we will have "changed our minds," and as best we can we will have put on the mind of Jesus. Jesus's mind was guided and formed by his fully-developed God-consciousness. The key virtues in Jesus were fully in alignment with his openness to God. By conforming our minds to the mind of Jesus, we will each develop and open our own God-consciousness, which will make us each more receptive to the truth and the love of God. This is our sanctification. To the believing Christian, this is the purpose and the ultimate goal of the truly human life.

Let us reflect on this. The final goals of a truly human life are to prepare oneself for union with God, and to make the world a better place. How, in the Christian view, is this to be done? I suggest that it is to be done by fully human natural processes. Jesus, a man, uniquely endowed by God but still a man, teaches us that we must change our minds, and struggle against our instinctive genetically-based urges and desires and against the wisdom of the world, the culture of sacrifice. He teaches us that we must concentrate our efforts on the development and practice of five specific key virtues, non-violence, non-judging, forgiveness, humility and detachment from possessions, and make use of persistent private prayer and reflection to accomplish these changes. This teaching has been passed down to us by generations of followers of Jesus teaching other followers of Jesus. If we have the courage to accept the challenge and persist in its practice, we put on the mind of Jesus and we open ourselves gradually to the influence of God. Becoming open to the influence of God and receptive to his truth and his love is what is traditionally called redemption. When, in answer to Jesus's call, we take up his challenge and try to put on his mind, his habitual attitudes and his way of looking at things, we participate in our own redemption. The work we do is human work at the highest level. We can and will change our minds and hearts, in the light of Jesus's teaching and example, if we begin and persist in the effort to make those changes. All of this is the exercise of natural human powers and capabilities.

We can call the exercise of these natural human powers and capabilities the grace of God, but that seems confusing to me. There is no need for hypothesizing an unseen and unproven "supernatural" level of life to describe what is really going on in the process of the redemption of mankind. The elements of the sacred, the magical and the mysterious are characteristics of religions of the culture of sacrifice, intended to cloak the lies and unrealities of such religions. They are not appropriate for the mature religion of Jesus, in which "everything that is now covered will be uncovered, and everything now hidden will be made clear."

Mt 10, 26. It is more fitting, and more consonant with the ways of God as we understand them, to believe that as much as possible of the redemptive activity of Jesus takes place on the natural level of human capabilities.

The economy of God, as I said in Chapter II, generally involves the least, rather than the most, direct intervention by God in the life and development of mankind. In the Kingdom explanation, this "least intervention" was the endowment of Jesus with full-developed God-consciousness, so that (a) he recognized the instinctive genetically-based behaviors men and women must learn to overcome, (b) he clearly saw the key points of vulnerability in the way of the world, the culture of sacrifice, and (c) he taught the key virtues which would directly oppose those instinctive behaviors, undermine the culture of sacrifice at its key points of vulnerability, and establish the Kingdom of Heaven on earth in its place. The rest of the process is a natural human process, under the generally non-interfering guidance and protection of the Holy Spirit. Complex theologies of grace and of the supernatural life were built up by thinkers who did not appreciate the power of human teaching, human learning, human effort and human example to change the world and to redeem mankind, in the light of Jesus's teachings and the example of his life. We should apply the principle of parsimony. Like the Ptolemaic theory of the movement of planets, which became obsolete when Copernicus discovered that the planets move around the sun, theologies of the "supernatural" life can be discarded, because they distract us from seeing how men and women really move.

Do not misunderstand me. I do not suggest, nor do I believe, that men and women can redeem themselves without the initiating activity of God, who freely gives men and women the gift of redemption and the gift of participation in that redemption. I simply suggest that (a) the redeeming gift, or grace, given freely by God, *is* the human life and teachings of Jesus, and (b) we receive this redeeming gift by natural means and participate in its action by natural use of our human abilities.

Sanctification—The Christian Community.

Being a Christian is not a solitary activity. The Christian has always needed community with other Christians, from the earliest days of Christianity. But for much of traditional Christianity, the lay person's participation in the Christian community has generally been passive. He or she comes to church services, listens to the reading of the scriptures, listens to a sermon from a member of the clergy, and receives communion in what is more a private devotion of many persons at the same time than a community activity. For the Christian who actively seeks to develop his or her understanding of Jesus's core teachings and of the key virtues, and to strengthen his or her ability to put them into practice, a more active role in a Christian community, and thus a Christian community which permits and encourages a more active role, is needed.

There are a great many different kinds of Christian community, and each Christian will have to find one, or several, Christian communities in which to participate, based on availability and his or her needs and abilities at the time. Without being prescriptive, I suggest that many of us may profit greatly from finding or organizing a Christian community which is both democratic and small.

As we saw in Chapter VIII, the earliest Christian communities were non-hierarchical, non-violent, non-judging, and detached from possessions. They were communities in which all members took an active part, each according to his or her gifts and abilities, without priority or precedence. Our model for Christian communities free from the corrupting influence of the culture of sacrifice should be those earliest Christian churches.

The earliest Christian communities were small groups, which met regularly in the homes of the members. My own experience tells me that the community activities which most directly develop one's understanding of Christian teachings and one's ability to apply them in the real world are the activities of talking about one's thoughts and concerns with a small group of people interested in similar development, and listening to the thoughts and concerns, the viewpoints and the advice, of the others in the group. For both of these reasons, I have come to believe that an important Christian community for many people will be what we now call a study group, a discussion group or a faith-sharing group. Such a group should be large enough to allow different viewpoints and insights, but not so large that not all of those present can participate in the discussion. Perhaps anywhere from a dozen to twenty-five or thirty people is the right number—not a group too large to meet regularly in the homes of its members, as the earliest Christians did. The group may well be a continuing community, meeting regularly over a period of years, so that a real bond of affection and mutual support develops and flourishes.

Such a Christian community might work out a schedule or syllabus of discussion topics for a period, with assigned readings for preparation. Its meetings would naturally include common prayer. And for many of such groups, the meeting would normally include a eucharistic meal, the Lord's Supper. As I do not believe that Jesus intended priests to intermediate between God and man, or to officiate at a sacrifice, so I see no reason why any member of the group, man or woman, perhaps the host or hostess, could not say the words of consecration over the bread and wine and distribute communion to the others.

The consecrated bread and wine, in the Christian eucharistic service, are the preeminent symbols of the presence of Jesus in the minds and hearts of the Christian community. This is a real presence. As the members deepen their understanding of and adherence to the teachings and the person of Jesus, and their love for one another, the real presence of Jesus becomes stronger and deeper. The bread and the wine are symbols of that presence. The presence of Jesus which means something to Christians is not his presence in the bread and wine, but his presence in the hearts and minds of the Christians gathered together. I believe that when Jesus said, "This is my body" and "This is my blood," he meant that the body of Christians gathered together in his name and in mutual love is his body and his blood. As Jesus said (in another context), "How could you fail to understand that I was not talking about bread?" Mt 16, 11.

The traditional Christian teaching that the bread and wine themselves are physically changed into the body and blood of Jesus is a relic of the period when the Christian Church was converting pagans by the thousands to Christianity, the period of the late Roman Empire and the Dark Ages. It was impossible at that time to teach all the converted pagans that magic has no place in Christianity, so the second-best route was taken. The pagans were permitted to believe in magic, as long as the objects of the magic were Christian magic. By magic I mean the belief that things themselves have powers, like amulets or charms, or that things can be changed by magicians into other things, which things when so changed have power. An example of the former is the power attributed to relics in the Middle Ages. The foremost example of the latter is the teaching that the bread and the wine themselves are physically and magically changed in substance. The symbolism of this distorted notion of the "real presence" of Jesus is unsavory and primitive; symbolically, it says that Christians gain strength by eating the flesh and drinking the blood of the man whose teachings they follow. This is truly symbolism from the culture of sacrifice. In any event, magic has no place in true Christianity. "How could you fail to understand that I was not talking about bread?"

There are continuing practical problems of maintaining small Christian communities like those described above, such as stability over a long period, attraction and introduction of new members, professional support and the provision of specialized services. The traditional Christian congregation or parish may well be perfectly suited to supply these needs. A congregation or parish is a stable and enduring institution in a way in which a study group cannot be. It can offer specialized services, such as the education of children and the continuing education of adults, which the smaller group can not. It can provide a larger community and a larger venue for public celebration of baptisms, marriages and funerals. It has a professional staff, which can provide professional counseling and special ministry to the troubled, the sick and the bereaved, and guidance in the formation and continuation of the study groups. It generally employs a professional pastor or rector, who preaches weekly to his or her congregation. But an ordained priest or minister will not be required for presiding at parish-wide eucharistic services or administering other sacraments; any member of the congregation trained in their administration could do so. Such a congregation should be self-governing, should recruit and select its own staff, and should be responsible for its own budget. If the congregation maintains an affiliation with a historic denomination which has bishops, the bishop should be elected by the people of the diocese, as was the practice in the early Christian Church.

For Roman Catholics, whether there is a useful function for the Pope and the Roman curia to perform in the service of local Roman Catholic communities is in my view an open question. Perhaps Rome can learn to facilitate communication between and among congregations and dioceses around the world, without unilaterally imposing its own views as to orthodox Christian teaching. Or perhaps the Roman curia's highest and best use is to care for and preserve a truly excellent museum in the Vatican. As it is unlikely that the Pope and his curia will either change or go away, it will be prudent for Catholics to bear in mind that if and when the people of any diocese or parish refuse to recognize the authority of the Pope to appoint and remove bishops and priests, the Pope will have lost his power over that diocese or parish.

The Sanctification of the World.

The core teachings of Jesus, if accepted and put into practice by Christians, will succeed in overcoming the culture of sacrifice. As Jesus promised, the Kingdom of Heaven will grow. "It is the smallest of all the seeds, but when it has grown it is the greatest of shrubs and becomes a tree, so that the birds of the air come and make nests in its branches." Mt 13, 31. But at present, the Christian Churches seem to have withdrawn from the world, and the responses of Christians to today's problems are uncertain. There are several reasons why this is so:

1.   There is a strong Christian tradition of withdrawal from the world, exemplified by the hermits, the monasteries, the convents and the groups of brethren like the Mennonites and the Amish which have withdrawn in entire communities from the world. Some of the teachings of Jesus can be read to encourage and support such withdrawal.

2.   The traditional specifically Christian mission to the world has been that of missions of conversion, following Jesus's last words to his disciples, "Go therefore and make disciples of all nations." Mt 28, 19. Missionary work has been one of the great and enduring historic accomplishments of the Christian church, from the work of St. Patrick and St. Columba to St. Francis Xavier to the heroic missionaries of the present day. But many Christians are ambivalent about missionary work in the modern age, for good reason. Christian missionary work in the last five centuries has often consisted more of bringing the secular values of Western culture to places where they had not reached than bringing the true Christian message. The Christian missions of the Spanish to the New World were accompanied by fire, sword, smallpox, and wholesale subjugation of the indigenous people. Our late-twentieth-century sensitivity to diversity of cultures and their preservation has meant that support for traditional Christian missionary activity is now somewhat guarded and qualified. There is a well-founded concern that Westernized Christianization of primitive peoples, challenging and uprooting their indigenous cultures and customary morality, may have done more harm than good; this is particularly evident in Africa.

3.   There is presently a sense of doubt among Christians, questioning whether the Christian message really makes a difference. In our own society, there are many good Christian people, but there are many good non-Christians as well. We do not see generally higher ethical standards or greater devotion to the common good in our society among Christians than among

secular humanists, and where on occasion we do, we are by no means sure that Christian faith has much to do with it. The historic influence of Christian values on Western societies over the last two thousand years has been profoundly influential in building the moral foundation on which these societies are based, but these values are now the values of the secular culture. For example, the American creed is the Declaration of Independence: "We hold these truths to be self-evident, that all men are created equal, that they are endowed by their Creator with certain unalienable rights, that among these are life, liberty and the pursuit of happiness." These are profoundly Christian values, now the foundation of our secular culture. Our world is still filled with problems, with evil and human suffering, but many Christians do not now see whether there is a specifically Christian answer or remedy for these problems. So Christians have frequently withdrawn from the world to a concern with and a pursuit of personal salvation.

But while much of Jesus's teaching speaks toward the personal salvation of his followers, much also speaks to the salvation of the world. Jesus said to his disciples, "You are the salt of the earth . . . . You are the light of the world. A city built on a hilltop cannot be hidden." Mt 5, 13-14. "The Kingdom of Heaven is like the yeast a woman took and mixed in with three measures of flour till it was leavened all through." Mt 13, 33. "Indeed, God did not send the Son into the world to condemn the world, but in order that *the world might be saved through him.*" Jn 3, 17. Jesus has thus clearly said that it is the mission of Christianity to change the world, and to save the world through him, and that the nature of that mission can be learned from his teachings.

As we have seen, Jesus directed his core teachings toward the replacement of the culture of sacrifice with the Kingdom of Heaven. The Christian Churches have historically adapted to the culture of sacrifice, and have not taught or practiced the core teachings. If the core teachings of Jesus were now accepted, and practiced, would that make a difference? Or, to put it another way, are there problems and evils in our present world which seem intractable of any known solution, to the resolution of which men and women who have cultivated the key virtues and core teachings taught by Jesus could make a significant contribution? Let us review the key virtues:

Non-Violence. The culture of sacrifice is dying throughout the world. The social utility of organized violence, and its capacity to bring peace, has rarely been so seriously questioned as it is now. Some examples of the failure of violence and its culture:

(a) Centuries of warfare among the great European nations culminated in the enormous destruction of the two World Wars. Since 1945, the nations of Europe have united, non-violent resolution of all European community problems prevails, and war between nations in Europe is no longer thinkable.

(b) Violence between nuclear powers can never be a rational solution to troubles. When a nation has the power to destroy all life on Earth, as the United States and Russia have, that power can never be used. Nuclear war between India and Pakistan, or between Israel and the Arab nations, is a real threat and would have unspeakably horrifying consequences. An alternative to violence must be found.

(c) At the time I am writing this, the United States has recently waged an undeclared war against the government of Afghanistan with its uncontested air superiority, and more recently, with Congressional authorization, an eager President has waged war against the government of Iraq, again trying to change the hearts and minds of a people by dropping large quantities of high explosive on them. Many people, both in America and abroad, have serious doubts about both the practical wisdom and the morality of these policies, and many fear that their most probable practical result will be to anger and harden the hearts of those who hate America and burn for the chance to take revenge.

The conventional wisdom, and the belief of most Christians, is that non-violence is impractical and unrealistic. We must retain the capacity to retaliate against attack, it is said. We must retaliate when attacked, or our power and willingness to strike back will not be believed. Evildoers will only respect force; only the application of power can control the Others (whereas we ourselves are always open to discussion and negotiation). We see where this leads in the conflict between the Israelis and the Palestinians. Each side repeatedly avers that retaliatory violence is its only option: "There is nothing else we can do."

The conventional wisdom is that measured and limited retaliation is justified and necessary. As we saw in Chapter VI, several evolutionary psychologists, in efforts to deal with the violence they found in the human condition, counseled measured retaliation, the *lex talionis* (an eye for an eye) or tit for tat. Four thousand years of experience with the *lex talionis* should have persuaded us by now that it does not and cannot work, certainly not when weapons of destruction have become so powerful. Controlled and limited violent retaliation requires an intellectual distancing from the emotions of a people under attack which would never occur. Were the calculating theorists of the nuclear standoff between the United States and Russia in the Cold War brilliant and tough-minded, with their contemplation of "mutual assured destruction," or were they, as the acronym suggests, just mad? Violence cannot be controlled with violence. Simply from a concern for human survival, many people have concluded that violence between nations makes no sense and can no longer have any practical justification. Girard puts it this way: "The definitive renunciation of violence, without any second thoughts, will become for us the condition *sine qua non* for the survival of humanity itself and for each one of us."[4]

The teachings of Jesus are clear as they can be. "Do not resist an evildoer. . . . Love your enemies and pray for those that persecute you. . . . All who take the sword will perish by the sword." Who is to say that non-violence is impractical and cannot work, when what we are presently doing is so clearly impractical and cannot work? If Christians study, absorb and accept Jesus's teachings of non-violence, and put them into practice, the world will change. The time is now. As Lincoln said, in proposing the

Emancipation Proclamation, "The dogmas of the quiet past are inadequate to the stormy present. The occasion is piled high with difficulty, and we must rise with the occasion. As our case is new, we must think anew and act anew. We must disenthral ourselves, and then we shall save our country." Non-violence has a mysterious and irresistible power over violence; this was shown by Gandhi and by Martin Luther King. The commitment of every Christian to non-violence will have impact, because non-violence is spread powerfully and effectively by the personal example of the thoughtful and committed adherent. I believe that only the root-and-branch opposition to violence found in the core teachings of Jesus can be the source of effective change.

As we resist violence with non-violence on an international scale, so we must resist it nationally and locally. The violence of men who beat their wives or children must be stopped, not by force, but by replacing the values of such men with the values of Jesus (to which some of them give lip service). The vengeful and retributive character of America's criminal justice system must be changed. Prosecutors and the media have made violent retaliation a primary goal of our criminal justice system. They call it "victims' rights," and retributive vengeance is called "closure." This is the way of the culture of sacrifice. Someone (not this author) needs to develop and publish a work on what kind of criminal justice system is consonant with a non-violent and non-vengeful society, so that we can make the changes necessary to administer a more humane and effective justice system.

I do not suggest that it is possible to eradicate violence completely from our society or from the world. For one thing, the effort must be put forth anew with each generation, as each person born into this world has violent behavior built into his or her genetic makeup, and there will always be some men and women who will lose control, or choose not to exercise it. But I believe committed Christians can make great progress in reducing violence, particularly communal or corporate violence, the kinds of violence that are built into our societal institutions and our common culture.

Non-Judging. In a way, non-judging, with its close ally forgiveness, is central among the key virtues. As Thomas Merton perceptively observed, most men and women can commit a violent act or acquiesce in violence only if they can first satisfy themselves in their own minds that the victim is different from themselves, and (unlike themselves) deserves the violence. Michael Ghiglieri pointed out that in warfare, killing the enemy must be justified in the mind of the soldier. If this cannot be done, the soldier will not fight, or he will go mad.[5] So judging, deciding that the other deserves pain and punishment, must precede violence. And non-judging will therefore prevent violence.

Non-judging is also closely allied to humility. The natural tendency to think that I am superior to others, or that my family, my school, my ethnic group or my country is superior to others, leads with almost imperceptible swiftness to finding fault with the others, then deciding that the others are not entitled to equality with me or my group, and then determining that the others must be subjugated to us by violence.

Because judging, criticizing and condemning the other is the way we channel our naturally-selected behavior of kinship loyalty and hostility to others, it is very difficult to control. Our minds play tricks on us to keep us from being truly tolerant and forgiving. For example, each of us holds convictions as to what life is about, and how life is to be lived. Non-judging does not mean that these convictions are not true and right, even though others do not share these convictions. Non-judging equally does not mean that we who hold these convictions can consider ourselves superior to those who do not. Non-judging requires careful and precise thinking and reflection. It requires intellectual independence as well as an interest in and a concern for those who are different from us. Jesus called us to lead lives of intellectual and emotional independence, maturity and discernment.

The Christian virtues of non-judging and forgiveness are at the root of the secular principles of tolerance and of the equality of all persons before the law upon which the Constitution and the laws of the United States are based. Much of the history of the United States is the narration of the continued effort of Americans to work out the consequences of these principles and to put them into effective practice; the Civil War was fought to end slavery, a manifest violation of these principles. There has been great progress in tolerance in America in the last hundred years. Prejudice against women, Catholics, Jews or African Americans which was expected and common in America in the early part of the twentieth century is simply not acceptable now. In this respect, the "good old days" were quite bad. But there remains much to be done. We are now faced more than ever before with the task of applying the principles of non-judging and forgiveness on a world-wide basis. Our country is frequently drawn into ethnic conflicts (Bosnia, Kosovo) and religious conflicts (Kashmir, the Middle East) throughout the world. It is tempting to the United States, given its unmatched military power, to judge who are the bad guys, the Others, and to drop bombs on them (and on all the innocent people in their vicinity). This cannot be the response of committed Christians.

Detachment from Possessions. From the Sermon on the Mount: "Do not worry about your life, what you will eat or what you will wear . . . . Look at the birds of the air; they neither sow nor reap nor gather into barns, and yet your heavenly Father feeds them." In our day, we can reflect on this teaching and shed some light on the virtue of detachment from possessions. To people in abject poverty, or refugees from famine, flood or war, every day is a day of constant worry about what they will eat, or drink, or wear. It should be a mission of Christians to alleviate, and ultimately remove, the scourge of abject poverty from the world, so that people of all nations will be free to pursue more important matters, and free to hear and follow the teachings of Jesus if they choose. In our time, for the first time in the history of the world, we have the power, the productive capacity, and the distributive means to do this. The key virtues of Jesus are interrelated: if the world makes any progress toward a culture of non-violence, vast sums now spent on armies and their equipment will be freed up for use in alleviating poverty. Our "war" should be a war on poverty throughout the world, not only because it is the only right thing to do, but because our own safety and freedom will not be secure until the people of the rest of the world have some property, and adequate food, drink, clothing and lodging, and thus a common desire with us to keep the world at peace.

It is not an easy or a simple task, as our experiences with foreign aid and domestic welfare programs have shown. It is difficult to keep foreign aid from being stolen by corrupt rulers of impoverished countries. It is difficult to supply food to the starving without destroying the livelihood of local farmers. It is difficult to provide welfare without making recipients dependent on welfare and incapable of becoming independent from it. But it must be done, and we need the teachings of Jesus to give us the confidence that it can be done. In the years of the depression, the Second World War, and the immediate post-war period, there was a spirit of sharing the burden in America, which brought a great many people out of poverty and into a decent life. In the last twenty-five years or so, the gap between rich and poor in America has widened, and continues to grow, and both foreign aid and domestic welfare have been cut back substantially. America needs a renewal of the Christian spirit of detachment from possessions.

Humility. Humility, according to Jesus, means that the rulers are not at the top of the hierarchy, but are servants of the people. "Whoever wishes to be great among you must be your servant . . . just as the Son of Man came not to be served but to serve." Much has been done in America to require service, not domination, from those whom we call our public servants, but much more needs to be done. Too many of our elected representatives are indebted to rich contributors or to special interests, or are able to use their own fortunes to buy public office. Internationally, the problems are even more difficult.

Many countries are still ruled by a military hierarchy, or a religious one, as in the days of the ancient culture of sacrifice, and it is generally these countries in which poverty and irrational inter-ethnic or inter-religious hostilities and hatreds are most deeply rooted. The key internal virtues taught by Jesus, detachment from possessions (which implies freedom from want), and humility (which implies freedom from hierarchies), are the virtues which make men free.

Final Reflections.

The core teachings of Jesus hold out to us not only the hope and promise of personal sanctification and salvation, but also the hope and promise of a better world. They must not only be believed and accepted, but we must put them into practice. As Jesus said, "It is not those who say to me, 'Lord, Lord,' who will enter the kingdom of heaven, but the person who does the will of my Father in heaven." Mt 7, 21. This is the task of Christians. This is the final overthrow of the culture of sacrifice, and the completion of the second half of creation.

I have set forth a natural and rational interpretation of the mission of Jesus. Fundamentalism, whether Christian, Islamic or whatever, is irrational, and is filled with belief in the constant interference of God in the ways of man. But fundamentalism, with its belief in magical interferences from God, and its obsession with external observances and rituals, is pagan in its roots; it is a survival of the culture of sacrifice which Jesus came to undermine and transcend. Fundamentalism does not understand the way God has chosen to deal with mankind. I have proposed in its place a human and rational set of understandings of the dealings of God with men and women. I propose a set of understandings which offers us greater personal challenges than any fundamentalist creed, and greater hopes and expectations for the maturation of mankind and for our final union with God.

I have set forth the reasons why the Christian Churches have not yet understood the mission of Jesus, and have not placed the core teachings of Jesus at the center of their own teachings. I have set forth what I believe is the true explanation of why Jesus came, and I have sketched the beginnings of some new thinking about what true Christianity, understood in the light of that explanation, can do in the world, if it is understood, practiced and applied. This interpretation of the mission and of the teachings of Jesus places a lot of trust and confidence in Jesus, but that is what Christians do. In light of the Kingdom explanation, can we hope that men can accomplish by application of Christian virtues in the future what two thousand years of Christianity have not accomplished? Yes, I think we can.

Am I suggesting that Jesus was just a social reformer, with a prescription for changing the world? No. Jesus came to change men and women, so that they could then be united with him, and through him with God. He sought to achieve this change by calling men and women to reject the culture of sacrifice and commit themselves to the practice of the key virtues. He intended that by means of such practice the God-consciousness of each person would develop and become the source of each person's guidance and control of his or her own self-consciousness and actions. Jesus understood, and said, that men and women so changed will change the world, and that by being so changed they will receive eternal life. Thus will be fulfilled Jesus's final prayer to his Father:

> "I have given them the glory you gave to me, that they may be one as we are one. With me in them and you in me, may they be so completely one, that the world will realize that it was you who sent me and that I have loved them as much as you loved me." Jn 17, 22-23.

Notes:
1. *Catechism of the Catholic Church* (Doubleday Image Books, 1995), Sections 153-54.
2. Branch, Taylor, *Parting the Waters* (Touchstone, Simon & Schuster, 1988), pp. 194-96, 259-63, *et passim*.

3. Merton, Thomas, quoted in *The New York Times*, October 21, 2001, p. A-16.
4. Girard, René, *Things Hidden Since the Foundation of the World* (Stanford University Press, 1987), p. 137.
5. Ghiglieri, Michael P., *The Dark Side of Man* (Perseus Books, 1999), p. 180.